To Bill
lots of love
april 2013
Trish
x x

Foreword by **Mervyn Davies**

I WAS PRIVILEGED AND HONOURED TO BE CAPTAIN of Wales during one of the most successful periods in Welsh rugby history.

We had some fantastic players during the 1970s with the likes of Gareth Edwards, Barry John, Phil Bennett, Gerald Davies, JPR and JJ Williams, and the Pontypool front-row not only becoming household names in Wales but world figures.

Playing alongside them was wonderful and we were able to win two Five Nations Championship Grand Slams and three Triple Crowns.

They were magnificent days but are just a part of the amazing story that is Welsh rugby.

The only other country where union is the No 1 sport is New Zealand. If Wales is doing well on the rugby field, industry bosses claim the feel-good factor reaches the work-place and productivity levels soar.

Rugby is that important. If Wales are going through a miserable period, the man and the woman in the street is also down in the dumps.

There have been so many ups and downs stretching back to the opening international, against England in 1881, it has been a real roller-coaster ride.

This potted history of Welsh rugby records the highs and lows from the first Grand Slam of 1908 to the World Cup flop of 2007. It is essential reading.

THE LITTLE BOOK OF
WELSH RUGBY

This edition first published in the UK in 2006
By Green Umbrella Publishing

© Green Umbrella Publishing 2008

Publishers Jules Gammond and Vanessa Gardner

Printed and bound in Italy

ISBN: 978-1-905828-46-3

Contents

Chapter 1

1881 - 99
The Welsh Passion for Rugby

THERE ARE ONLY TWO NATIONS where rugby union is truly king, where the passion for the game runs deep and where it is the very heart and soul of the people.

No other country can match Wales and New Zealand for the fervent interest the magical 15-a-side game generates among the public, whether it's in Cardiff or Wellington, Llanelli or Dunedin, Swansea or Auckland.

Rugby has to play second fiddle to soccer in most of the other great rugby powers. The round-ball game rules the roost in England, France and even South Africa, where it has a huge following among the majority black population.

In Australia, the only nation to have twice lifted the ultimate rugby prize, the World Cup, union is some way down the pecking order. There's Aussie Rules, rugby league and cricket, to mention but a few.

Competing with other sports for column inches in the newspapers and television coverage isn't something union has to contend with in Wales, unlike its Celtic cousins Scotland and Ireland. The Scots are mad for their soccer while the Irish have Gaelic football and horse racing. Rugby is played by the middle and upper classes in

THE WELSH PASSION FOR RUGBY

LEFT Coal mining started from a very young age in Wales

Ireland, Scotland and, to a fair degree, England but it's a working class game in Wales, the sport of the masses.

Perhaps the reason why union became such a hit with the Welsh population can be found in the culture and history of Wales in the late nineteenth century. It was at the heart of the Industrial Revolution, an engine room for Great Britain producing millions of tonnes of coal from the valleys of South Wales and iron in its vast factories.

The popularity of rugby might have been helped by the defiant, independent streak of the Welsh. It gave them a different outlet to soccer-mad England to proudly parade their talent and ability on the world stage, a chance to project and express themselves.

Wales has bred natural rugby players, people so at ease with having the ball in their hands, and their mesmerising touches have captivated the world. Gareth Edwards is widely acknowledged as the greatest player in history while the likes of Gerald and Mervyn Davies, JPR Williams, Bryn Meredith, Barry John, Phil Bennett and Cliff Morgan would be prime contenders for an all time World XV.

Union had taken place for some years in Wales before the country played its first international against England at Blackheath on 18 February 1881. The growth of the sport had been prompted by students returning from the great universities and schools the other side of Offa's Dyke.

Wales was famous for its industrial and educational innovators and that skill was quickly transferred to the rugby field as it played a key part in

LEFT Coal mining started from a very young age in Wales

THE WELSH PASSION FOR RUGBY

France, Scotland and Ireland. There were amazing scenes in Cardiff after they clinched it by beating the Irish at the Millennium Stadium.

Rugby, you see, has always been an emotional affair for the Welsh. When an unofficial representative side made its bow in the Test area at Mr. Richardson's Field in England and were promptly clobbered by the equivalent of 82-0 in today's scoring system, there was outrage in Wales, which led directly to the formation of the Welsh Rugby Union.

The South Wales Football Union was in place but the gravity of the defeat against the Red Rose provoked an intense debate in the heartland of Welsh rugby. History suggests the men in red who won the very first caps awarded by Wales were members of a team put together by Richard Mullock, a member of a well-known Newport family, but which failed to contain many of the country's best players.

developing the sport. The country became famous for the so-called Welsh way of playing, a cunning, fast, skilful, running and passing game which bedazzled opponents and spectators with its wizardry.

Only last year that style was apparent as Wales thrilled by winning the Six Nations Championship with a high-risk brand of attacking play that netted them a Grand Slam with victories over World Cup holders England, Italy,

Although Mullock might not have intended it at the time, his efforts prompted Wales to come together under one banner. A meeting was called at the Castle Hotel, Neath on 12 March 1881 and drew delegates from far and wide. There was Bangor from North Wales, Brecon and Llandovery from Mid Wales, Lampeter, Llandeilo and Llanelli from West Wales, Merthyr from the heart of the South Wales valleys, Pontypool from the Gwent valleys and city clubs Cardiff, Swansea and Newport.

Somewhat ironically, considering the venue of Wales' first foray in the international arena, the gathering was chaired by a Swansea captain with the surname of Richardson.

The outcome was the establishment of a governing body now more commonly known as the WRU. It needed a secretary and Mullock, who had borne the brunt of the anger for the Welsh performance at Blackheath, was duly appointed and served for 11 years. His vision of Wales being at the cutting edge of the growth of the sport convinced the representatives of the clubs he should be at the forefront of the revolution.

The presence of learning centres Llandovery, Brecon and Lampeter at that historic meeting highlighted the importance of students and educational establishments to rugby during the early years. Seven of the inaugural Welsh team went to university at either Cambridge or Oxford, including the captain James Bevan.

His was a fascinating story. He was born in Melbourne, Australia but was orphaned at the age of eight when the *London*, a ship carrying his wealthy Welsh-born parents Down Under following a trip to Europe, sunk during a fierce Atlantic storm in the notoriously dangerous Bay of Biscay.

Young James was sent back to Wales to be cared for by relatives at Grosmont, a village near Abergavenny and practically on the border with England. He went to the upper-crust Hereford Cathedral School and Cambridge University. Bevan made just one appearance for Wales, that opening foray against England, when they conceded 13 tries, seven conversions and a dropped goal.

BELOW Wales coach Graham Henry at the Millenium Stadium, Cardiff, venue for the opening match of the 1999 Rugby World Cup, between Wales and Argentina

Wales also faced county sides like Gloucestershire and Somerset and went down narrowly against the North of England at Newport in January 1882. That improved performance paid dividends later that month when they beat Ireland at Lansdowne Road, Dublin, crossing four times.

Only four of the players who had started against England, CH Newman, GF Harding, Frank Purdon and WD Phillips, had been retained for a fiery fixture. Ireland only had 11 players at the final whistle, two having departed with injuries and two having walked off in disgust after disagreeing with the decision

ABOVE Welsh supporters gather to watch Newport, 1906

of the Welsh umpire, WRU secretary Mullock. Substitutes weren't allowed in those days.

Wales' presence on the fledgling international stage and the advent of the South Wales Challenge Cup struck a chord with the public and the clubs quickly had a large and vocal support base. Roots were put down in the

community and, very often, the rugby club became the focal point for the village or town.

There was fierce tribalism and intense rivalry. The 1970s might have witnessed the birth of the soccer hooligan but rugby had similar problems on and off the field, nearly a century earlier. Fighting between players was commonplace and there were even instances of referees being assaulted by angry spectators. The cup competition was temporarily disbanded. It wouldn't be the only time.

England, and more specifically a winger called Gregory Wade, who went on to become Premier of Australian state New South Wales, proved too hot for the Welsh defence when the first international was staged in Wales, at St. Helen's, Swansea in December 1882.

His debut was a hat-trick spectacular. Rugby was still in its infancy and teams had generally relied on one-up rugby where the ball-carrier ran until he was tackled but England provided a new dimension by passing their way to a comfortable success. Wales quickly cottoned on and became innovators, experimenting with the four three-quarter system, consisting of two centres and two wingers, which was to become the norm.

Despite their willingness to improvise, Wales continued to struggle on the big stage. Their next outing was in Scotland, at Raeburn Place in Edinburgh, and it ended in a defeat by three goals to one goal, 21-7 in modern terminology.

The clash took place on a bitterly cold day in January 1883. Forward Tom Judson scored the Welsh try with Charles Lewis converting. It was also the setting for the Bridie mystery. Ron Bridie had reportedly been selected for Wales but was a Scotsman and never appeared. It is believed George Harding took over from him. Why this happened has never been firmly established.

The following season saw Wales play three international matches, against England at Leeds, Scotland at Newport's Rodney Parade ground and Ireland, in the first Test to take place at Cardiff Arms Park. England were again too good but the gap was closing. Wales got on the scoreboard through North Walian Charlie Allen, Lewis converting, but England replied with three touchdowns.

Half-back Billy Gwynn was hailed as

the first Welsh passer of the ball and attracted rave reviews, but his skill and unorthodoxy were unable to prevent them slipping to defeat against Scotland, during a close and gripping affair.

Wales notched up another victory against Ireland, scoring tries through Tom Clapp and Billy Norton. The Irish had shown up two players short and had to draft in Frank Purdon and HM Jordan from Welsh clubs Swansea and Newport. Bill 'Buller' Stadden put over Wales' first drop goal.

Nicknames were common during those formative days. There was 'Monkey' Gould, 'Pontymister' Williams,

ABOVE Wales team group: (back row, l-r) J Taylor, WH Evans, George Williams, Caesar Jenkyns, John Jones, AW Pryce-Jones, EJ Hughes, FT Evans; (middle row, l-r) Billy Meredith, Joseph Davies, goalkeeper J Trainer, Harry Trainer, William Lewis; (front row, l-r) Charles Parry, D Jones

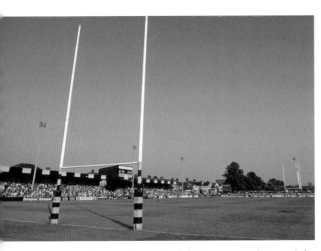

national career lasted 13 years and he gained 27 caps, a remarkable figure considering the lack of fixtures.

Although today's players might believe criticism is a new phenomenon it was rife in the nineteenth century with Gwynn, who was to succeed Mullock as WRU secretary in 1892, being pilloried for his wild passing as Wales lost by a goal and four tries to a goal and a try (27-12).

There was a scoreless draw between Scotland and Wales in Glasgow on 10 January 1885. Progress was being made with the Dragons getting closer to getting their first major scalp. Unfortunately, there were setbacks during the journey to greatness with England once again proving too strong the following year.

'Rev. Charlie' Newman and Percy 'The Sparrow' Phillips.

Characters abounded on the field but there wasn't much harmony off it. The Welsh selectors arranged a trial but only one of the West XV turned up because of a row over selection methods.

Gould, who became one of the most famous players to don the red jersey, made his debut at full-back against England at St. Helen's in 1885. His inter-

ABOVE Stradey Park
home of Llanelli

Ireland weren't on the fixture list as acrimony resulted in a temporary stand-off in relations between the two countries. Scotland remained, however, and their forwards were too good for Wales at Cardiff Arms Park.

England were next to come to Wales, to the West Wales cauldron that is Llanelli in January 1887. Wales held them to a draw with neither country posting a point. The match was switched to the adjoining cricket pitch at Stradey Park because the rugby ground was semi-frozen. Snow and sleet fell during the second half and a crossbar collapsed with Arthur Gould, who had acquired his nickname of 'Monkey' for his climbing prowess, replacing it.

Wales went to Scotland and suffered a

ABOVE Arthur Gould

right old thumping with George Lindsey scoring a record five tries. Questions were asked of the Welsh defence and it failed to answer them although its cause was not helped by the loss of half-back Jem Evans and Billy Douglas being a passenger following an early injury.

Fixtures resumed with Ireland in 1887, the match taking place on neutral soil at Birkenhead on Merseyside, not because of past differences but in order to cut costs for the financially-pressed Irish. Gould's dropped goal, which was equal to three tries back then, proved vital as they just managed to stave off a terrific fight back by their opponents. Under the modern scoring system, Ireland would have been triumphant.

Scotland were edged out at Rodney Parade with Gould, playing at his home club and in front of 7,000 fanatical supporters, having a starring role. Debut-maker Tom Jenkins got the Welsh try as they raced to their first win over the Scots, who had already

secured two Triple Crowns.

'Buller' and 'Monkey' missed the trip to Dublin. The absence of Welsh rugby's two stars and the loss of Ned Roberts with an ankle injury proved conclusive as Wales suffered their first reverse against the Irish.

England did not play that season so Wales faced a touring team. New Zealand Maori were the first to visit the British Isles and went down by the equivalent of 17-0. They went on to copy the Welsh four-three-quarter system. The Maori played a staggering 107 matches during the tour.

There was friction in the Welsh camp that season over selection, with anger in the west at the inclusion of just three players from the area. It erupted in a huge bust-up before the clash with Scotland following the withdrawal of Norman Biggs. His decision prompted others to follow suit and they went down in a snowstorm at Raeburn Place.

Wales lost to Ireland at St. Helen's and their 1890 campaign got off to a bad start when they went down at home to the Scots. A new points-scoring system, put forward by Wales, had been adopted by the International Rugby Board, and they arrived on the international scene

by beating England 1-0 at Dewsbury. A try was worth a point and 'Buller' got it following a clever line-out ploy.

An away draw with Ireland was followed by defeats against England and Scotland in 1891. Wales accounted for the Irish but it was their only victory in seven matches. Those disappointments were soon forgotten as Wales beat England 12-11 in Cardiff with Swansea full-back Billy Bancroft landing the decisive penalty.

Scotland were beaten 9-0 in Edinburgh. Expectations soared in Wales and nearly 20,000 saw them dispose of Ireland 2-0 at Stradey Park on 11 March 1883, Gould's brother Bert getting the vital touchdown, to secure a first Triple Crown.

Wales never reached the same heights during the rest of the decade but the popularity of rugby in the Principality continued to rise with a then record crowd of 40,000 watching the clash with Ireland at the Arms Park in 1899. It was a sign of things to come.

ABOVE The New Zealand Maori faced Wales in 1887, seen here in 1916 performing the 'haka'

Chapter 2

1900 - 14
The First Golden Era

SUCCESS CAME THICK AND FAST for Wales as the twentieth century was ushered in with a glorious brand of rugby. There were three Grand Slams, an amazing six Triple Crowns and victories over the feared New Zealand All Blacks and Australia before the start of the horrific and bloody First World War in 1914.

Wales had won only 16 out of 46 matches played during the previous century. There had been three draws but 27 defeats. Fortunes took a drastic upturn during what was acclaimed as the first Golden Era of Welsh rugby.

There were 43 triumphs in 56 games, a remarkable success rate which highlighted just how far Wales had come in a short period of time and the quality of athlete it was already producing.

Undoubtedly, the coal mines and the ironworks, which were dotted on the South Wales landscape, were a contributory factor. Life was particularly harsh in Wales. Working conditions were extreme but they bred hard and strong men. Fitness of players was virtually guaranteed because the jobs many occupied automatically honed bodies

LEFT Wales team group: (Extreme back row) Linesman Ack Llewelyn; (Back row, L-R) Tom Williams (WRFU), JF Williams, George Travers, D Jones, W Joseph, Rhys Gabe, WRFU President Sir JTD Llewelyn ; (Middle row, L-R) CM Pritchard, Jehoida Hodges, Willie Llewellyn, Gwyn Nicholls, Bert Winfield, Cliff Pritchard, AF Harding; (Front row, L-R) Teddy Morgan, Dicky Owen, Percy Bush

into peak condition.

The working class participation in the game was a distinct advantage as it ensured a ready-made production line of players possessing the physical attributes to propel Wales towards the top.

Arthur Gould was no longer on the scene following a bitter row between Wales and the International Board over his status after a WRU supported testimonial fund was set up for him. The union presented 'Monkey' with the title

THE FIRST GOLDEN ERA

deeds of his house in recognition of his career but rival countries branded him a professional. There was a threat to Wales' international future but Gould defused the situation by retiring.

Without his selfless action, Wales might have been cast into the wilderness and that first Golden Era lost. Perhaps Gould realised exciting times and a new generation of stars were about to be unleashed on the international stage. The legendary Billy Trew made his debut as Wales kicked off the twentieth century against England at Gloucester's famous Kingsholm venue on 6 January 1900.

The mercurial talent appeared on the wing although his best positions were centre or at outside-half. Dick Hellings got the other. The Llwynypia forward

was made of granite and was a real tough cookie, playing almost the entire match with a fractured arm. Skipper Billy Bancroft converted both and kicked a penalty in a 13-3 triumph.

Another Llwynypia product, dynamic winger Willie Llewellyn, grabbed two tries as they overran Scotland in front of 40,000 at St. Helen's, Swansea. Fellow great Gwyn Nicholls, who had a set of gates named after him at Cardiff Arms Park, also crossed. So did 'Pontymister' Williams during a 12-3 success.

A Triple Crown was waiting for Wales but it took a tremendous effort to bring it home from Balmoral, Belfast. The critical moment came in the second-half when Newport half-back Lou Phillips burst away from a line-out. Nicholls was in support and powered past a defender before passing to George Davies.

The Swansea

ABOVE Willie Llewellyn had an amazing strike record with 16 tries in 20 caps

RIGHT Astute captain Billy Bancroft made an amazing 33 consecutive appearances for Wales over 12 years

centre dived over but, for his troubles, was kicked in the mouth and knocked out. He was carried off and it wasn't until later that he realised his try had given Wales a 3-0 victory. The astute Bancroft had ordered a change of tactics and his judgement was crucial in delivering glory.

Wales' defence of the Triple Crown began with a 13-0 triumph over deadly rivals England the following year. That man Nicholls, it was claimed, carried six defenders with him over the try-line. 'Pontymister' Williams, a forward who knew where the whitewash was located, got his second in three games with Newport's Jehoida Hodges adding another.

Facing Scotland at Inverleith was the next mission for Bancroft's men. They were full of confidence and red-hot favourites but, as has happened to so many fancied Welsh sides since, came home with their tails between their legs.

Wales suffered a considerable blow when orchestrator Phillips damaged a knee early in proceedings and was unable to contribute much afterwards. This time Bancroft was accused of blundering by not moving the lame Phillips away from half-back.

There was evidence of Scotland's fast, rucking game, which has become their hallmark, as their fiery forwards laid the foundation for a pulsating 18-8 success en route to a third Triple Crown. Llewellyn Lloyd and George Boots, whose surname was more akin to that of an American Wild West gun-fighter, got the Welsh touchdowns with Bancroft adding a conversion.

The selectors made changes, introducing the famous Swansea half-back pairing of Dicky Owen and Dick Jones against Ireland at St. Helen's on 16 March 1901. They were to form a partnership in 15 internationals, a record that stood until Gareth Edwards and Barry John broke it in 1970.

There were parallels between Owen and Edwards: the former is believed to have invented the reverse pass while the latter was a master of it.

ABOVE Dicky Owen formed a famous Welsh half-back pairing with Swansea team-mate Dick Jones

Wales were at the forefront of change. The WRU successfully campaigned for the differential penalty and changes to the scoring method with the awarding of points for tries and goals.

Owen was to win a record 35 caps, a figure that stood for more than half a century, but admitted he struggled during his debut against the passionate Irish. Wales were outscored 3-2 in tries but the goal-kicking of Bancroft proved crucial. He converted Billy Alexander's brace. Ireland were unable to match his accuracy.

Bancroft retired after an amazing international career spanning 12 years and 33 appearances in a row. Nicholls, now with Newport, took over the captaincy in 1902 and Wales got their campaign off to a positive start with a thrilling 9-8 victory over England at Blackheath's Rectory Field.

Wales trailed 8-3 at the interval but snatched success when full-back Jack Strand Jones created a superb touchdown for Llanelli team mate and centre Rhys Gabe. The large Welsh contingent

in the crowd erupted with joy. There was controversy, however, when Owen conned the English into giving a penalty away by dummying to pick the ball up at a scrum. England back-rower Bernard Oughtred was caught offside and Jones put over the dropped goal amid allegations of unsportsmanlike behaviour.

A 40,000 crowd showed up at Cardiff Arms Park for leg two of Wales' assault on the Triple Crown. It was played in a gale and Scotland skipper Mark Morrison claimed he made a mistake by electing to play into the wind. But the scoreline suggested otherwise with the Dragons 14 points ahead despite being up against the elements.

Llewellyn and Gabe each crossed twice with Strand Jones converting one. Interest in the subsequent clash with Ireland at Lansdowne Road went through the roof and it was one of the first all-ticket international matches.

As so often in history, Ireland had a formidable pack but lacked finesse in their back division. Wales just about held them up front and had too much skill and guile in their back division.

Try-machine Llewellyn darted over and tricky outside-half Llewellyn Lloyd

made a diagonal run to the corner while Nicholls, who had dropped a goal, used his strength to power in. Alfred Brice converted one and a second Triple Crown was the property of Wales. The blistering start to the century had continued.

Wales had to cope without shoulder injury victim Nicholls when they tackled England at St. Helen's on 10 January 1903. Veteran Tom Pearson took over leadership duties but lasted just 25 minutes before his match came to a crunching halt when he was laid out by a tackle from Bert Gamlin.

Hodges moved from the pack to the wing and netted an amazing hat-trick of tries as they won 21-3. George Travers made his debut. It was a marvellous achievement in its own right because he had been plucked from tiny Newport club Pill Harriers. But the selectors' faith in him was vindicated as he went on to play another 24 matches for Wales and became the world's first specialist hooker.

Scotland and Wales were the two strongest nations in the Home Championship at that point and their clash in Inverleith was billed as a Triple Crown decider. The furious Scots were desperate to avenge their defeat of the previous season and ripped into Wales, winning 6-0.

Wales responded to the criticism that followed by thumping Ireland 18-0 at Cardiff Arms Park. Llewellyn and Teddy Morgan both crossed twice, with Gabe and Brice joining them on the scoresheet. Boots suffered a broken collarbone early on but somehow summed up the determination to play on until half-time.

The following season opened with a 14-14 draw with England at Welford Road, Leicester, Bert Winfield's late goal staving off the threat of a Welsh defeat. Wales were angry with the refereeing of Crawford Findlay. It wasn't their only

LEFT George Travers
BELOW Centre Rhys Gabe was a prolific try-scorer for Wales

THE FIRST GOLDEN ERA

disagreement with the Scottish official.

Scotland's bid for a fourth Triple Crown foundered when they went to Swansea on 6 February 1904, Gabe, Dick Jones, Morgan and Brice all getting tries for Wales during a 21-3 walloping.

Crawford was portrayed as the villain for controversially disallowing what would have been a late winning try from Jones in Belfast a month later as Wales were edged out 14-12 by Ireland.

England were struggling to compete with Wales and were unable to contain the wily half-back partnership of Jones

Ireland in Swansea.

The Irish took the lead but nippy Mountain Ash outside-half Wyndham Jones dummied his way through the green defence for a wonderful try. Then he put Morgan over for another, George Davies converting both. Wales had taken the third Triple Crown of the century.

They had bigger fish to fry later in the year in the shape of New Zealand. Wales hadn't been beaten at home for six years but the imposing All Blacks arrived at the Arms Park on the back of a record 27 victories in a row.

The ground was full an hour before kick-off as a record 47,000 crammed in, and they witnessed a memorable and controversial encounter which is still debated to this day.

Owen was targeted by New Zealand but had the satisfaction of devising the move that deceived the All Blacks' defence. His legendary reverse pass freed Cliff Pritchard, who linked with Gabe to put Morgan over for what transpired to be the decisive try.

New Zealanders still maintain Bob Deans scored an equalising touchdown but it was ruled out by Scottish referee John Dallas on the grounds the centre

and Owen as the home side powered to a 25-point success in 1905.

Llewellyn, who had been appointed captain in the absence of the injured Nicholls, took his try tally to 16 with two more as Wales beat Scotland 6-3 to set up a Triple Crown decider with

had been stopped just short of the line. Morgan, assisted by Gabe, was credited with tackling him and Wales had won 3-0. Even on his deathbed, Deans insisted he had made the line and grounded the ball before being pulled back.

A month later, in January 1906, Wales were opening their defence of the Triple Crown against England in Richmond. Showing that they were still prepared to experiment despite their outstanding successes, Wales cut the number of forwards from eight to seven, putting an extra man in their backs. The match also heralded the arrival of the first specialist front-row.

The three-man front-row was a resounding hit and was adopted by the rest of the world, but fielding a back division consisting of eight players was scrapped for good the following year as opponents took advantage of having an extra forward at the scrummage.

Initially, the radical plan was a success as England were thumped 16-3. Scotland were also beaten despite getting the better of the Welsh pack. Wales reverted to eight forwards as they attempted to wrap up the championship in Belfast. However, Ireland, despite finishing with 13 men, outplayed them and won 11-6.

Nicholls' final appearance came as Wales succumbed 11-0 at home to South Africa after coming off second-best at forward and failing to flourish at half-back with Owen and Cardiff's Bush lacking cohesion.

Despite that setback, Wales were far too strong for the poor English at St. Helen's in 1907, running in six tries after re-introducing their seven forwards-eight backs plan. But it was dispensed with permanently following a 6-3 defeat in Scotland.

Trew was captain but refused to play against Ireland because a Swansea team mate had been banned by the WRU for dissent so Gabe took over leadership duties. Cardiff winger Johnnie Williams raced over for a hat-trick as Wales piled up 29 unanswered points.

France entered the championship in 1908, just as the Welsh team was blossoming into possibly the country's best of all time. There were Grand Slams and Triple Crowns that year, the following and in 1911.

Wales began their blitz by beating England 28-18 in Bristol. The 25,000 crowd didn't see much though because the ground was shrouded in thick fog. Gabe set a captain's example with two of their five tries. It was a lot harder against Scotland, Trew and Williams crossing as they hung on to win 6-5 at St. Helen's.

The French found the going tough in Cardiff, Wales winning 36-4 while Ireland were beaten 11-5 in Belfast.

Australia made their bow at the Arms Park on 12 December 1908 but a penalty from Bert Winfield allowed Wales to win a roughhouse of an encounter 9-6. Wales, with Trew now at the helm, were unbeaten that season. Only Scotland, in Edinburgh, provided a major test of their resolve.

Wales opened the following campaign with their 11th consecutive victory, a record that still stands, by demolishing Test rookies France 49-14 at St. Helen's. Curiously, that fixture took place on New Year's Day 1910.

The winning run came to an end as unfancied England notched up their first victory over Wales in 12 years, marking the opening of Twickenham with a spectacular try from wing Fred Chapman. It came from the kick-off and caught the Welsh defence cold.

They regrouped to dispose of Scotland, in a Cardiff mudbath, and Ireland, but were pipped to the championship by resurgent England. The arch-rivals were the two best sides in 1911 with Wales having to dig deep to win 15-11 at St. Helen's, a late try from Joe Pugsley snatching the spoils.

Scotland were thumped 32-10, France 15-0 and Ireland 16-0 during a Triple Crown decider. It was Wales' seventh Triple Crown and their last for 39 years as the good times rolled to a grinding halt.

There was another defeat against South Africa, 3-0 in 1912, and Wales also went down at home to England prompting radical changes by the selectors. The break out of war scuppered any hope of an immediate revival.

BELOW Bob Deans died maintaining he had grounded the ball for the All Blacks

Chapter 3

1915-26
Lean Times

THE FIRST WORLD WAR HAD brought death, poverty, depression, misery and despair. Wales suffered from the conflict along with Five Nations Championship rivals England, France, Ireland and Scotland.

Times were desperate with the Great War, as it was more commonly known, raging on the battlefields of France and Belgium. It claimed the lives of millions, including top sportsmen, as the trench warfare took an awful toll. There was no hiding place with victims coming from every strata of society.

Eleven Welsh internationals were killed in the madness. They included highly rated half-back Lou Phillips and Cardiff winger Johnnie Williams, who had raced over for a hat-trick of tries against Ireland in Dublin in 1910.

Richard Williams, Charles Taylor, Charlie Pritchard, Dai Westacott, Dick Thomas, Phil Waller, Brinley Lewis, Billy Green and David Watts were the other fatalities.

Wales played one match during the war, an uncapped military international against the Barbarians at Cardiff Arms Park in 1915. In reality, it was an exercise to boost recruitment for the Welsh Guards, who were seeking 1,000 new soldiers, with speeches made at half-time encouraging spectators to join up.

The Welsh team was captained

Tom Parker. But a Barbarians side mostly made up of English players but also containing two Irish and one London Welsh representative, proved too strong, running in six tries during a 26-10 victory. Ivor Davies and Bryn Lewis replied for Wales, with Clem Lewis landing a dropped goal.

There were 13 debut-makers when big-time rugby resumed following the end of the war, Wales hosting a New Zealand army team at St. Helen's, Swansea on 21 April 1919. Only skipper Glyn Stephens (Neath) and Newport half-back Walter Martin had played pre-war.

A crowd of 30,000 had turned up eager to watch after suffering

by Reverend Alban Davies, an army chaplain who won seven caps, and contained debut-makers Dan Callan and from the rigours of the Great War but it was an error-laden encounter. Perhaps that was to be expected with both sides

ABOVE New Zealand
pictured in the 1920s

struck by nerves and Wales having never played together previously.

Jerry Shea, who was to emerge as one of the most colourful characters Wales had produced, put Wales into the lead with a penalty but New Zealand hit back through the big boot of Jack Stohr. He kicked two penalties, one a monster

effort from half-way, to give the Kiwis a 6-3 victory at the end of a dour and disappointing contest.

Blood had been spilled with Martin carried off clutching a cut to his head, which led to the New Zealanders' boot studs being examined. They were found to meet regulations in place at that time.

Defeat was a taster of what was to come for Wales. Rugby was hit by the recession that was taking hold. It resulted in many potential players leaving the country as the search for work and financial security took them far and wide. Welsh talent popped up all over the place.

Wales also became fertile ground for raiding parties from the north of England. Rugby League, following the separation of the Northern Union from the Rugby Football Union, and the advent of the 13-a-side code without line-outs, rucks, mauls and containing dubious scrums, was gaining in popularity.

It also paid players and was a perfect solution to the plight facing those with talent but struggling to find work in Wales. Although there was criticism of some of those who headed north, one couldn't really blame them for turning professional because they simply didn't have a choice with prevailing circumstances dictating.

League, as it grew and prospered throughout Yorkshire, at that time a county larger than Wales, and Lancashire, offered a similar environment to union in Wales.

It was a working class game centred on the coalfields of Lancashire and Yorkshire so it felt like home from home to many of the Welsh prodigies who succumbed to the lure of a lump sum to sign for clubs like Wigan, St. Helens and Leeds and the prospect of healthy pay packets.

Scouts employed by the rugby league outfits kept a close eye on the union fields of South Wales, casting their net extensively in the search for talent. They continued to poach Welsh internationals until the 15-a-side code was declared open in August 1995, allowing the payment of players and prompting bigger salaries than the league boys were getting.

The methodology of the league clubs was simple: signing Welsh stars even though they had never played the 13-a-side game created interest and drew larger audiences. They would pay a Welsh player significantly more money than a person with compatible ability and who had been brought up on league.

Conversely, the likes of Castleford, Widnes, Hull Kingston Rovers and Bradford rarely targeted England union internationals because such a move would not have generated the same interest as signing a foreigner.

LEAN TIMES

To some degree, it's the same story in Wales nowadays with Welsh union clubs more akin to offering bumper wage deals to foreigners than to home-grown products.

The exodus of talent was a significant factor in the trials and tribulations suffered by Welsh rugby in the 1920s. A bright start, when the Five Nations Championship resumed, might actually have contributed to the downfall because it resulted in more players being targeted by the professionals from 'up' north.

Showman Shea was responsible for 16 of Wales' 19 points as they disposed of England with something to spare at St. Helen's on 17 January 1920. Shea, who was accused throughout his career of being selfish and wasting opportunities by disregarding team mates in better positions, dropped two goals, kicked a penalty and, for good measure, converted his own try to go through the scorecard.

Cardiff right-winger Wickham Powell got Wales' other try as the 40,000

spectators went wild with excitement. It was a regular occurrence for them to invade the pitch at the end of matches and they certainly did so that day with Shea and popular Swansea full-back Joe Rees, a crowd favourite, being chaired off amid joyous scenes.

Shea had initially been capped while

goals repeatedly but many of his critics seemingly failed to realise Wales finished with 13 men after losing 37-year-old captain Harry Uzzell and Aberavon forward Jim Jones through injury.

When Wales lined up against France in Paris 10 days later, Shea was missing. Not because the selectors had reacted to the criticism but through his ability in the boxing ring. He was booked for a bout and could not make the journey across the English Channel.

Wales won 6-5 in highly contentious circumstances. Powell and fellow winger Bryn Williams (Llanelli) crossed for unconverted tries. France replied with a try from Adolphe Jaureguy, converted by Toulouse star Philippe Struxiano. They thought they had secured their first victory over the Welsh when skipper Struxiano claimed he had gone over in the corner following a quickly-taken line-out. English referee Colonel Craven signalled a try but disallowed it after seeing the raised flag of the Welsh touch judge, who explained it should have been a Wales throw-in.

Foul weather seemed to be a regular hazard in those days with Wales defying a waterlogged pitch at Cardiff Arms Park to

with minnows Pill but transferred to Newport. His adulation by the Welsh public lasted less than a month because he was publicly castigated following a shock 9-5 defeat to Scotland at Edinburgh's Inverleith ground. Shea was accused of putting his own interests ahead of the team by attempting to drop

demolish Ireland 28-4. Williams became the 10th Welsh player to score a hat-trick of tries. Albert Jenkins, Jack Whitfield and Parker joined him on the scoresheet with the former and Jack Wetter each landing two conversions. Jenkins also put over a sweet dropped goal as they shared the championship with England and Scotland.

The following campaign resulted in Wales posting a won two, lost two record. They had gone to Twickenham with a jumbo pack and in a buoyant mood but were mercilessly swept aside as they suffered their heaviest defeat for 26 years.

New captain and play-maker Wetter injured his right knee with a quarter of the game gone and was a passenger for the remainder. Casualties mounted with three-quarters Tom Johnson and Jack Jones suffering painful injuries. Centre Johnson damaged a hand while Jones heroically lasted to the end despite fracturing a collarbone five minutes before the interval.

Pontypool star Jones was part of a record-holding family for, along with 'Ponty' and 'Tuan', they remain the only trio of brothers to have been capped by Wales. Twenty-seven pairs of brothers have appeared for the Dragons.

England's confidence soared following their 18-3 success and they went on to lift a fifth Triple Crown. The match was also Shea's last for Wales, who brought in four new caps against Scotland.

But neither the enthusiasm of Frank Evans, Paul 'Baker' Jones, Tom Roberts and William Bowen, nor a near 50,000 crowd at St. Helen's could fire them to success.

There were two lengthy stoppages caused by spectators encroaching on the pitch and concerned Scotland captain John Hume threatened to take his team off permanently. But he was glad they stayed on because they went on to post a 14-8 victory.

Wales made more changes against France, handing debuts to Cross Keys full-back Ossie Male, Llanelli centre Harry Davies and Swansea half-back Tudor Williams. Tries from Jack Williams and Wilf Hodder, with Jenkins landing two penalties, saw them maintain their unbeaten record against France.

They finished the championship on an encouraging note with a 6-0 success in Ireland and began 1922 in sensational style by blasting England aside 28-6 in a huge upset at Twickenham.

Showing they remained innovators,

BELOW Wales v England in 1922

LEAN TIMES

ABOVE March 1926: The referee and team captains on the pitch before the start of the Wales versus Ireland Rugby International at Swansea. From left to right, WL Crawford, the Irish captain, referee BS Cumberlege and Rowe Harding, the Welsh captain

eight tries, through Hiddlestone, Jack Whitfield, Bowen, Bobby Delahay, Frank Palmer, Cliff Richards, Parker and Islwyn Evans with Joe Rees converting two.

Evans, with a close-range dropped goal, secured a draw with Scotland in the dying minutes at Inverleith. The power of the Welsh pack set up an 11-5 victory over Ireland at St. Helen's and they were crowned champions with an 11-3 triumph in France. Whitfield crossed for the fourth time of the campaign. Will Cummins and Evans also scored with Jenkins nailing a conversion.

However, Wales' fortunes plummeted and they recorded just three victories in 15 fixtures between 1923-1926. There was just one win in 1923, 16-8 against France during a violent meeting at St. Helen's which culminated in the referee summoning the French Federation's secretary on to the field to issue a final 'cool it' warning.

England had scored in a record 10 seconds at Twickenham, through flying forward Leo Price. Skullduggery was common and Wales were on the receiving end on this occasion with Tom 'Codger' Johnson being laid out by a kick to the head. Ambrose Baker suffered badly bruised ribs, Joe

Wales came up with a novel way of halting the English plan to continue with the running rugby which had brought it seven victories in a row. The Welsh selectors decided to field two flankers for the first time, in debut-makers Tom Jones and Dai Hiddlestone, and they had sensational matches.

Despite the muddy conditions, spectators were able to identify players because both teams had numbers on their jerseys for the first time in a championship match. Wales rattled up

Thompson had three teeth knocked out and Dai Davies needed stitches to stem the flow of blood from an ugly gash under his left eye.

The Welsh crowd generously carried Scotland skipper Archibald Gracie off the field after he sunk Wales with a breathtaking try two minutes from the final whistle at Cardiff Arms Park. Wales went down 11-8 and finished a dismal campaign with the Wooden Spoon following a 5-4 defeat in Ireland, their first against the Irish in 11 years.

It didn't get any better the following year with Wales again having to salvage some pride against France. The French were still rookies in 1924 and, like Italy today in the Six Nations Championship, initially found the going tough and wins rare.

Wales didn't have much to shout about themselves, losing against England at home for the first time since 1913. England went on to notch up a seventh Triple Crown, equalling the Welsh record. Wales did introduce a real star in the shape of famed Llanelli flanker Ivor Jones.

'Flying Scot' Ian Smith scored three of Scotland's eight tries as they inflicted Wales' heaviest defeat since the 1880s. Worse was to come when brothers Tom

BELOW The Wales squad, 1924

LEAN TIMES

RIGHT Wales vs Scotland, 1927

and 17-year-old Frank Hewitt both scored as Ireland triumphed in Wales for the first time in 25 years.

The slump meant only three Welshmen, Rowe Harding, Vince Griffiths and Marsden Jones were selected for the British and Irish Lions tour of South Africa which followed. A fourth player, Harold Davies, joined them as a replacement. The only occasion where Wales have almost fared so badly was when just five made the 1993 party which went to New Zealand.

The size of the 1924 contingent was a stark contrast to 1908, when 13 made the trip to Australia and New Zealand after Wales clinched the Grand Slam.

New Zealand extracted ample revenge for their controversial defeat in 1905 by running in four tries during a resounding 19-0 victory at St. Helen's in November 1924.

It was veteran Wetter's final appearance, a collision with All Black legend George Nepia laying him out. New Zealand proved invincible during the tour. Hiddlestone had enlivened pre-match proceedings by leading a Welsh war dance in response to the haka.

Wales' backs didn't have the class to

turn pressure into points against England at Twickenham in January 1923. They lost 12-6 but, with more finesse, might have won. Next up they faced one of the finest Scotland sides in history and lost 24-14 at St. Helen's. Smith did the bulk of the damage with four tries, two of them coming after 60-metre sprints. It was ranked as

one of the best matches between the countries. Scotland went on to win their first Grand Slam, a feat they have only repeated twice since.

Wales had beaten France 11-5 in front of their smallest crowd (28,000) in years but lost to Ireland. It was the first time Ireland had recorded three consecutive victories over Wales. Making it worse, it

was a record Irish win against them, 19-3 at Belfast's new Ravenhill ground.

Some pride was restored the following season with a 3-3 draw against England at Cardiff Arms Park, a narrow 8-5 defeat at the hands of Scotland on their first visit to Murrayfield and with encouraging, albeit it narrow, victories over Ireland and France.

Chapter 4

1927-45
Mixed Fortunes

WALES WON JUST NINE OF THEIR 32 games between 1923-30 and it wasn't until 1950 that a Grand Slam, let alone a Triple Crown, was pocketed.

Thirty-nine long years passed before they managed to repeat the feats of 1911. Their best achievement during the intervening period was a magnificent 13-12 victory over the 1935 New Zealand All Blacks at Cardiff Arms Park.

Nevertheless, even during the dark days of the 1920s, there had been some notable performers, people like Harry Uzzell, Jack Wetter, Dai Hiddlestone, Rowe Harding, Albert Jenkins, Wick Powell, Watcyn Thomas, Archie Skym, Ned Jenkins, Ossie Male, Ivor Jones, Bobby Delahay and showman Jerry Shea.

Powell was the prototype for Terry Holmes and recent cap Mike Phillips, in that he was bigger than the traditional scrum-half, was packed with power and was a right handful to would-be tacklers. He was also a useful defender, as was proven when he made his international debut on the wing in 1926.

Powell occupied that position twice more and was credited with nullifying the considerable threat posted by Scotland winger Ian Smith. The 'Flying Scot' had helped himself to a total of seven tries in his two previous encounters with Wales but found his way to the line blocked by the imposing figure of the London Welsh player.

Windsor Lewis and club-mate Powell

George Andrews.

Wales, though, failed to follow up that performance, losing 5-0 to Scotland at Cardiff Arms Park. It was their fifth successive defeat to the Scots, who scored the only try of the game through David Kerr after Harding was dispossessed.

It was the final appearance of 18-times capped Delahay, who high-

formed a promising half-back partnership against England at Twickenham in January 1927. Wales were unlucky to lose after outscoring their opponents 2-1 in tries and playing for 65 minutes a man short after Newport forward Dai Jones fractured a bone in a shoulder.

A try and goal from a mark by England captain Len Corbett, backed up by 'Erb' Stanbury's conversion just about saw off Wales. The Welsh tries were scored by British and Irish Lions tourist Harding and fellow winger

lighted the versatility of players in the early part of the twentieth century by winning caps at scrum-half, outside-half and centre. He was a late call-up for the match. Powell and Lewis were selected but the latter withdrew through injury. The selectors asked Powell to stand down because they preferred to field a club duo at half-back, Delahay and Cardiff team mate Gwyn Richards.

Powell and Lewis returned against France at St. Helen's. Male was replaced

RIGHT The Wales squad for the match against Scotland: (Back row, L-R) Edwards, Bobby Jones, Thomas Hopkins, Sydney Hinam, Steve Lawrence, Emlyn Watkins, Howell John, George Andrews; (Front row, L-R) Lewis, Dai Jenkins, Arthur Cornish, Wick Powell, Albert Stock, Rowe Harding, Dai Jones, Bill Everson, unknown; (Seated, L-R) Ron Herrera, Bobby Delahay

as captain by Powell, who became the 17th of an unprecedented 20 players to lead Wales in the 1920s. Even during other dark periods, such as in the 1980s and 1990s, Wales never changed their captain with such frequency.

The French were still the whipping boys of European rugby and conceded seven tries as Wales put together their best attacking movements of the championship to win 25-7. Surprise, surprise, it rained most of the match and the pitch was near to being waterlogged.

A glance at the home clubs and colleges of the Welsh team on duty that day highlights there was still an opportunity for players to get capped from smaller outfits. Crumlin forward Billy Williams was in the line-up that day but it was before the formation of the Merit Table. When it was set up some years later, it was almost impossible to get capped from a team outside it, other than an educational establishment like Cambridge or Oxford University, or Cardiff College of Higher Education, now called UWIC.

The formation of a league structure in 1990 cut opportunities further with only players from the top 12 clubs getting a look in. Now, of course, the professional structure has been streamlined into four

regions and it would be a stunning coup for a player to be capped from a semi-professional club.

The Welsh selectors, in the 1920s, didn't have the benefit of a league structure, television and video replays. They had to do the legwork in an effort to snare the best players. That meant racking up the miles, usually by train because motorised road transport was still in its infancy.

Seeing the national team pick up the Wooden Spoon for the fourth time in five seasons, courtesy of their 19-9 defeat against Ireland at Lansdowne Road, in March 1927, must have been a harrowing blow for them, especially with their charges being accused of a lack of effort. The Irish, with centre George 'The Rocket' Stephenson and left-wing Jim Ganly each crossing twice, even managed to overcome the loss of hooker Allan Buchanan just before the

interval with injury.

Being a Welsh fan, let alone a selector, was a gloomy business. In November of the same year Australian side the New South Wales Waratahs, who reached the final of the crack southern hemisphere

Super 12 tournament in 2005, which has since been expanded to 14 teams, gave Wales a harsh lesson.

The Waratahs had beaten Ireland and France but had gone down to Scotland and England. However, they were still far

MIXED FORTUNES

too good for the ailing Welsh, controlling virtually every facet of a one-sided contest as they cruised to an 18-8 success, outscoring their hosts 4-2 in tries at a subdued Arms Park.

Wales played with a lot more fire when they began their 1928 Five Nations campaign against England at St. Helen's, establishing an immediate edge at forward. But a stumble by Harding allowed Red Rose right-wing Bill Taylor to score the try that was ultimately the difference between winning and losing. Harding wasn't forgiven for his mistake, losing the captaincy and his place in the team. He never played for Wales again.

More bad weather, a gale and heavy rain, helped Wales overcome their Murrayfield jinx. They won the toss and elected to play with the wind. Jenkins, Dai John and John Roberts touched down with Male twice converting as they beat Scotland away for the first time in 15 years. It was also their opening success at the new home of Scottish rugby.

Unfortunately, it was a momentary lift for union in Wales. They proceeded to crash to a 13-10 home defeat against Ireland at the Arms Park with calls being made to drop the entire team. In fact, the pack had been more than a match for the men in green and were retained en bloc for the Easter Monday trip to Paris.

However, only Powell, Male and Roberts retained their places in a revamped back division. Powell reverted to scrum-half with Roberts moving to wing from centre in place of him. Cardiff's Gwyn Davies made his debut at right-wing but the result was calamitous, a first defeat against France. It was their 15th meeting. The only solace for Wales was that they were the last of the home nations to lose to Les Bleus. The French managed to achieve an historic 8-3 triumph despite being reduced to 14 men for most of the match after losing Andre Camel to a shoulder injury.

Wales made a sweeping nine changes when they opened their 1929 glory bid at Twickenham on 19 January and their resolute determination restricted a superior England, who had won a record eighth Triple Crown the previous season, to a five-point winning margin.

It was a signal that Wales were improving and they didn't lose again in the championship, beating Scotland and France before drawing in Ireland. Back play was back in vogue after the forward-dominated years that blighted the club game in the Principality, and the Wales back division sparkled with a number of handling movements.

Aggressive centre Harry Bowcott

made a considerable impact during his debut in the 14-7 success over the Scots, who went on to win the championship, at St. Helen's. It was the first time Wales had triumphed against them on Welsh soil in 15 years. Roberts, with a double strike, Harry Peacock and Guy Morgan scored the tries as the Welsh selectors and the public breathed a hefty sigh of relief.

Wales attempted to repeat their running and passing tactics against France at the Arms Park on 29 February but found the going difficult on a wet and greasy surface. Both tries were grabbed by forwards, Neath's Tom Arthur and Cardiff's Bob Barrell, with Swansea's Dai Parker converting one.

There weren't the neutral touch judges of today with the power to draw the attention of the referee to foul play and matches could be no-holds barred affairs. International rugby wasn't for the faint-hearted and the clash with Ireland in Belfast was such an affair. At times, it resembled a street

LEFT (L-R) Harry Bowcott makes a point to his fellow British Lions selector Des McKibbon

fight as both sides waded into each other, boots and all, during a brutal war of attrition.

The intensity of the battle resulted in four Welsh forwards requiring attention with Arthur dislocating a thumb and new cap Arthur Lemon dislocating a finger. Oh, the score was 5-5!

More battles occurred during the following season's clash between the nations, which went down in history as one of union's most violent matches. A French victory would have given them their first Five Nations Championship and they were fired up for the Easter Monday 'bloodbath'.

Off-the-ball punches were thrown as Wales refused to succumb to the intimidatory tactics of their opponents. Rugby seemed to be the last thing on the players' minds as they engaged in open warfare. Newport hooker Hubert Day's lip was left dangling from his face after he was punched in the mouth.

BELOW
Claude Davey

It required nine stitches to repair the wound.

Wales' national newspaper the *Western Mail* wrote "For sheer wanton brutality and savagery this match can surely never be approached in the annals of rugby football."

Perhaps the French would have been better off concentrating on the rugby because they went down 11-0. Skym scored the sole try, with Powell and Morgan each putting over dropped goals. It was also the debut of the 'sledgehammer' tackler, Swansea centre Claude Davey.

Wales had again started the tournament badly, looking lethargic as they lost 11-3 to England at the Arms Park. The Dragons performed better at Murrayfield but were defeated in gut-wrenching fashion when a dropped goal from outside-half Herbert Waddell ensured Scotland came out on top 12-9.

It was the final Wales appearance of skipper Ivor Jones, who years later became a president of the Welsh Rugby Union. The man who replaced him at the helm, Penarth's Jack Bassett, proved a colossus with his tackling reputedly preventing Ireland from scoring three tries. Wales clung on to win

12-7 and deny the Irish a first Triple Crown since 1899.

Jones, despite being dropped by his country, was picked by the British and Irish Lions for their tour of New Zealand and Australia. Bassett, Bowcott, Parker, Tommy Jones-Davies, Jack Morley and H. Poole, of Cardiff, who was never capped by Wales, took the Welsh representation to seven.

Living with the Lions that summer rubbed off on the rest of the Wales squad the following year because they won the championship for the first time in nine years in 1931. A Grand Slam and Triple Crown were denied by an 11-11 draw with England at Twickenham during their season-opener.

There was a real tale of heroism in their next fixture against Scotland, in front of an all-ticket crowd of 50,000 at the Arms Park. Pack leader Thomas fractured a collarbone but refused to go off, staying on to score a vital touchdown in the 13-8 triumph. Morley and Ronnie Boon also crossed with Bassett hammering over two conversions.

A snowstorm swept St. Helen's when France arrived in February and they folded in the bitterly cold conditions as Wales kept warm with seven tries. It was the last match between the countries for 15 years, a breakaway by 12 French clubs from their national federation resulting in a curtailment of fixtures.

The fearsome tackling of Bassett and Davey was crucial in the 15-3 championship winning success against Triple Crown-chasing Ireland in Belfast. It was a torrid encounter with Ireland centre Morgan Crowe led off with concussion before the interval. The

ABOVE Jack Bassett, Wales captain

Welsh also sustained casualties with a dazed Powell spraining an ankle, Bassett suffering a head wound and Ned Jenkins suffering a 'stinger' injury. He damaged a nerve in his neck and was temporarily partially paralysed.

European kings Wales were unable to beat South Africa later in the year, going down 8-3 on a St. Helen's pitch almost covered in water by a deluge. It poured down so heavily the playing of the national anthems was scrapped.

There was a three-way share of the 1932 Five Nations Championship,

MIXED FORTUNES

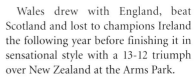

ABOVE
Viv Jenkins
BELOW
Haydn Tanner

between Wales, Ireland and England. A freak dropped goal by Ronnie Boon helped Wales to their first win over England in 10 years. The depression that had afflicted the world economy was a contributory factor in a crowd of just 30,000.

Wales remained on course for a Triple Crown after beating Scotland 6-0 in Edinburgh but were defeated 12-10 by Ireland at the Arms Park. Bassett had a nightmare match, being at fault on two of the Irish tries, and was never picked again.

Wilf Wooller, aged 20, and Viv Jenkins were unleashed by Wales in 1933, against England, but it turned out to be the Dragons' only success of the campaign.

Defeat against England marked the opening of the 1934 season and a new grandstand at the Arms Park. The English went on to win the championship with Wales runners-up after beating Scotland and Ireland.

Wales drew with England, beat Scotland and lost to champions Ireland the following year before finishing it in sensational style with a 13-12 triumph over New Zealand at the Arms Park.

Schoolboy star Haydn Tanner made his debut when he replaced Powell at scrum-half but the omens didn't look good when hooker Don Tarr dislocated his neck with Wales 12-10 down. The All Blacks had led through a try from Nelson Ball but Wales hit back through skipper Davey and wing Geoffrey Jones, Jenkins converting both.

Mike Gilbert slotted a dropped goal for New Zealand and converted Ball's second try to put them ahead. But Wales struck back with Wooller, who was to captain Glamorgan at cricket, broke away and kicked ahead. The bounce of the ball eluded him but Jones was on hand again for the decisive touchdown.

With their confidence buoyed, Wales won the 1936 Five Nations crown. Their match with England at St. Helen's was a 0-0 bore remembered more for the presence of Russian prince Alexander Obolensky in the Red Rose line-up.

Cliff Jones, perhaps the best Welsh outside-half of an illustrious bunch which has supplied tactical genius, was star of the show as they beat Scotland 13-3 at Murrayfield. He created Wooller's try and scored a gem himself.

There was mayhem before and during the championship decider with Triple Crown-chasing Ireland at the Arms Park. Fire hoses were turned on sections of an estimated 70,000 crowd, 14,000 more than the number permitted, when spectators rushed and broke down the gates. People, in fear of their lives, spilled over the railings and stood 15-deep along the touch-lines. Dozens were taken to hospital for treatment after being trampled in the stampede but, miraculously, nobody was killed.

Wales won the match 3-0, full-back Jenkins, later to become rugby correspondent of *The Times*, kicking the decisive penalty.

Wales went from heroes to zeros in the following campaign when they suffered a humiliating whitewash. Defeat in Scotland denied them a Triple Crown in 1938, a year which marked the injury-enforced retirement of Jones at just 24.

LEFT
Wilf Wooller

And Jenkins called it a day after they lost 3-0 to England at Twickenham as war loomed in 1939. Tanner was the architect of a 11-3 success over Scotland in Cardiff and they upstaged another potential Irish Triple Crown party with a 7-0 triumph at Ravenhill.

Chapter 5

1946-53
Pioneers

RIGHT Wales team group: (Back row, L-R) Gordon Wells, Ray Prosser, Rhys Williams, John Faull, Roddy Evans, Don Devereux, Haydn Morgan; (Middle row, L-R) Lloyd Williams, Cyril Davies, Malcolm Thomas, Clem Thomas, John Collins, Terry Davies; (Front row, L-R) Bryn Meredith, Cliff Morgan

WALES HAS BEEN BLESSED WITH visionary administrators. There were just 11 secretaries of the Welsh Rugby Union in the 121 years before the appointment of a professional management board and a chief executive at the helm.

The reign of each secretary averaged 11 years. Amazingly, its first, Richard Mullock, lasted exactly that length of time when he was in charge of affairs between 1881-92.

The former mayor of Newport became known as the 'Founding Father' of the WRU. He had expertise in business and was already one of Wales' leading sports administrators when the governing body was formed at the Castle Hotel, Neath on 12 March 1881.

Mullock, a member of Newport's most well-known families, was experienced at setting up organisations and was the ideal candidate to oversee the humble beginnings of the WRU.

He was involved in three sections of Newport Athletic Club – the rugby club was started by that body in 1874 and he was also its first secretary.

Mullock was a pioneer: he served on the general committee of the Amateur Athletics Association after helping found that organisation in 1880. He was secretary and treasurer of the WRU, joint secretary of Newport Cricket Club, and a cricket and rugby umpire – those were the days before they were called referees.

The WRU took six years to report its first profit, of £23 in 1887. That was the year when the International Rugby

Board was formed. Wales were founder members. Guess who was one of their delegates? The remarkable Mr. Mullock.

His successor at the WRU, Billy Gwynn, only lasted four years but presided over Wales' first Triple Crown in 1893. His reign might have been brief but you couldn't say that about the man who took over from him, Captain Walter Rees.

He assumed control in 1896 and kept his hand on the tiller for an incredible 52 years, until 1948. Rees had seen two

World Wars, on-field success and despair, and presided over unprecedented growth and popularity before he called it a day.

Examination of his record highlights his genuine leadership qualities and ability. He was appointed secretary of Neath in 1888 and a year later was elected as a member of the WRU's match committee.

It didn't take influential figures at the union long to realise this man was an organiser and decision-maker. As they pointed out, he was a captain who had been trained in the art of directing operations.

There were a mere 50 member clubs of the WRU when he sat in the secretary's chair for the first time. It was a paid role and he certainly justified his salary. The number had risen to 104 when he stepped down, an increase of more than 100 per cent.

Rees was in charge throughout the first 'Golden Era' of Welsh success in the international arena and watched gate receipts grow tenfold to £10,000. But that was just part of the story, this remarkable man somehow found the time to run for Neath Borough Council.

He was duly elected and his popularity is such he became its mayor in 1905. Rees also managed to fit in a trip to South Africa in 1910 with the British and Irish Lions as one of their two managers, and he also sat on the IRB for decades.

Rugby in Wales owes Rees and WRU president Horace Lyne, who worked in tandem with him, an enormous debt of gratitude. The pair each spent nearly 60 years serving their sport at various levels. Lyne was president between 1906-47, stepping down aged 86. Rees resigned a year later, aged 82. Amazingly, they died within a month of each other in 1949.

When Lyne, who had helped Mullock at Newport Athletic Club, retired in July 1947 he was the last surviving member of the original International Rugby Board.

Lyne, a forward who was capped six times for Wales between 1883-85, was also chief fire officer of Newport for the best part of half a century, was given the Freedom of the borough and was a member of the governing body of the Church in Wales.

Fittingly, he was awarded the MBE. His legacy lives on because he bequeathed the trophy given to him by the WRU to commemorate his life presidency back to it and it's now the Challenge Cup.

The reign of Rees and Lyne drew to a close just after the resumption of full international rugby in 1947, following the end of the Second World War. There had been a seven-year break caused by the 1939-45 conflict.

Three Welsh caps, Cardiff's Maurice Turnbull, Bedford's Cecil Davies and Newport's John R. Evans were killed in action in the Second World War. Eleven lost their lives in the First World War of 1914-18. Rather incredibly, prop Davies was the 478th player to be capped by Wales and Evans the 479th.

France's 15-year exile from the European title race ended when the Five Nations Championship was re-introduced in 1947. Wales and England met in the opening match at Cardiff Arms Park. England edged out Wales 9-6 but they ended up sharing the crown.

There were just two survivors from the team that had faced Ireland eight years earlier, skipper Tanner and Llanelli full-back Howard Davies. Of the 13 new caps, Newport sprinter Ken Jones, who won a medal at the 1948 London

Olympics, Neath forward legend Rees Stephens, and Cardiff trio Bleddyn Williams, Dr. Jack Matthews and Billy Cleaver, became household names.

Stephens and fellow debut-maker, Cardiff forward Gwyn Evans, got the Welsh tries in front of a crowd of 43,000. Attendance was restricted because of war-time bomb damage to part of a stand at the Arms Park.

Williams had made his bow at outside-half but switched to centre, becoming one of the best of all time, against Scotland. That allowed Pontypridd's Glyn Davies, fresh from school, to make his debut and he orchestrated a 22-8 triumph, Wales' biggest over the Scots since 1914 with his balanced running.

Davies benefited from having the experienced and astute Tanner inside him as the men in red flourished with five tries. Jones showed his exceptional pace by racing in for two. Williams, Cleaver and Llanelli's Lew Williams got the others. Tough Cardiff forward Bill Tamplin achieved folklore status by playing on despite suffering a dislocated wrist.

And the Welsh pack leader kicked the huge penalty which allowed them to beat France 3-0 at Colombres, Paris on 22 March. Although it was the first clash between the countries since 1932, little seemed to have changed.

Cardiff's Cliff Davies,

one of the best prop forwards in the world, had a finger bitten almost to the bone by a 'hungry' French mouth. Newport lock George Parsons was picked but was sent home by the WRU when it heard rumours he was negotiating with rugby league clubs. A year later he headed north, probably still angry at missing out on a cherished cap.

Wales, yet again, denied Ireland, who had the famed Jack Kyle at outside-half, a Triple Crown when they beat them 6-0 in the St. Helen's mud. The match had been due to take place three weeks earlier but was postponed because of a frozen pitch. Top-notch Newport flanker Bob Evans crossed with Tamplin adding a penalty.

Tamplin, who took over the captaincy when Tanner chipped an elbow bone, kicked both penalties in the six-point defeat of Australia at the Arms Park in December 1947. John Gwilliam, who was capped from Cambridge University, Edinburgh Wanderers and Gloucester, made his debut and was later to become one of Wales' most revered skippers.

A crowd of 73,000 at Twickenham watched England and Wales draw 3-3. The Welsh got the only try of the match, through master-finisher Jones but had another disallowed.

Jones, Williams and Matthew all crossed during the 14-0 success over Scotland at the Arms Park but they were unable to prevent France winning for the first time on Welsh soil, 11-3 in arctic conditions at St. Helens, a fortnight later. It might have been cold but, predictably, it was a

ABOVE
Cliff Davies, 1956
LEFT
Lewis Jones, Llanelli

RIGHT Wales' Jack Matthews (R) touches down for a try

hot-tempered affair with punch-ups and pitch invasions which held up play.

Wales were unable to prevent Ireland picking up a first Triple Crown in 49 years when they were beaten 6-3 at Ravenhill, Belfast. A sidestepping run

from Williams had levelled matters but forward Jack Daly's burst sealed victory for the Irish in front of 32,000.

Ireland proceeded to complete the Grand Slam, still their only one in history, and won three championships in four attempts during a magical period inspired by the legendary Kyle and a fiery pack of forwards.

Despite possessing talented players like Williams, Cleaver, Davies, Tanner, Stephens and Gwilliam, Wales took time to mature as a team. In fact, the side of the late 1940s, early 1950s were a bit like coach Mike Ruddock's Grand Slam winning team of last season in that it went through a long development process before they became championship winners.

Silky stepper Davies inspired Wales to a 9-3 victory over England at Cardiff Arms Park. Left-wing Les Williams touched down twice with debut-maker Alun Meredith grabbing the other. Remarkably, Newport hooker 'Bunner' Travers was recalled after a 10-year absence.

Davies came down to earth with a bump at Murrayfield as Scotland's spoilers wreaked havoc, coming out on top 6-5. Wales lost 5-0 to Ireland at St. Helen's and 5-3 against France

in Paris. That was the redoubtable Tanner's 25th and final Test match.

Clem and Malcolm Thomas had made their debut against the French and went on to become stars. But they were overshadowed by the arrival

BELOW (L-R) Wales' Ken Jones touches down to score a try before England's William Hook can tackle him

of Lewis Jones on the international scene in January 1950. Aged 18 years and nine months, he was the original running full-back. A rapier-like counter-attack created a try for prop Cliff Davies. It was a sign of things to come although, unfortunately, much of his career was spent in rugby league, where he became a 'great'.

Wales won 11-5, their first success at 'Twickers' in 17 years and only their second in 40, and they were en route to a first Grand Slam and Triple Crown since 1911. They ground out a 12-0 win over Scotland at St. Helen's, Malcolm Thomas and Jones getting the tries, and a 6-3 triumph over Ireland at Ravenhill.

Jones's try had been cancelled out by a penalty from George Norton and the game looked to be heading for a 3-3 draw when feared Pontypool forward Ray Cale secured a turnover. Jones threw a long pass and Thomas squeezed in at the corner.

Unfortunately, celebrations turned to despair when 80 Welsh fans died when their aircraft crashed while landing at Llandow Airfield, near Cardiff. It was the world's worst civil air disaster up to that time.

The Last Post was played by five buglers before the clash with France at the Arms Park a fortnight later. There was a subdued atmosphere as Wales led 5-0 at the interval but they opened up in the second-half to win 21-0. Jones bagged a brace of tries with Matthews and supreme line-out jumper Roy John getting the others.

Not surprisingly, rejuvenated Wales supplied the bulk of the Lions touring party that went to New Zealand and Australia. Fourteen players headed Down Under, including Bleddyn Williams, Matthews, Lewis and Ken Jones, Thomas, Cleaver, Rex Willis, Evan, Stephens, John and Newbridge tearaway Don Hayward. They won both Tests against the Wallabies but failed to muster a win in New Zealand.

Wales looked to be on course for more glory in 1951 after crushing England 23-5 at Twickenham. Matthews (2), Thomas (2) and Jones all crossed. Perhaps they became over-confident and complacent when 20,000 fans followed them to Scotland because it turned into the 'Murrayfield Massacre' as they suffered a shock 19-0 hammering.

The selectors dropped Glyn Davies and brought in the brilliant Cliff Morgan at outside-half as they held eventual

ABOVE John Gwilliam,
Steele Bodger's XV

RIGHT Gareth Griffiths,
WC Ramsay's
International XV

OPPOSITE RIGHT
Cliff Morgan

champions Ireland to a 3-3 draw in Cardiff. Gwilliam was dropped and they went down 8-3 in France.

South Africa faced Wales at the Arms Park the following season and might have been there for the taking but Morgan, in a rare blemish, kicked too much ball away. Just like the 2005 clash with New Zealand, it was billed as the unofficial world championship. The result was the same: victory to the southern hemisphere with the Springboks of 1951 winning 6-3. Williams scored a cracker of a try for Wales but it wasn't enough.

Gwilliam had been brought back as captain and they stormed to another Triple Crown and Grand Slam. England were accounted for first, 8-6 at Twickenham, after Wales recovered from a six-point deficit. A Morgan break created Jones's first and the winger turned on his after-burner for his second.

Willis fractured his jaw but stayed on

as they beat Scotland 11-0 at the Arms Park. Jones got a try in that and in the 14-3 triumph over Ireland at Lansdowne Road. Morgan was the star of the show with his exciting running while Wales had a gem of a flanker in Pontypool's Allen Forward. Clem Thomas and Stephens also made the try-line.

An injured Morgan was missing when they wrapped up the championship with a 9-5 win over France at St. Helen's. Lewis Jones kicked two penalties while Alun Thomas dropped a goal.

Hopes of a back-to-back championship evaporated in their first game of 1953

when they lost 8-3 at home to England, who went on to be crowned kings of Europe.

Williams (twice) and Jones scored tries during a 12-0 victory over Scotland at Murrayfield, wing Gareth Griffiths crossed during the 5-3 win against Ireland at Swansea and got all the points with two more in the notable 6-3 triumph over the French in Paris.

New Zealand were next up, at the Arms Park on 19 December 1953. Television viewers - it was the first Welsh home match to go out live – saw a classic encounter between the two most passionate union countries in the world.

Bill Clark got the All Blacks try, Ron Jarden converting and adding a penalty goal as they led 8-5, Sid Judd having gone over for Wales, and Gwyn Rowlands converting.

Time seemed to be running out for Wales when flanker Clem Thomas, seeing his path blocked by Kiwis, noticed unguarded territory the other side of the pitch and put in a pin-point cross-kick for that man Jones to pounce for the decisive try. It became the most famous of his 17 Test tries. Wales had won 13-8. It was their last victory over New Zealand.

Chapter 6

1954-68
Facing up to the Southern Hemisphere

ONE OF WELSH RUGBY'S ODDITIES is that Wales didn't embark on their first tour until 1964. During the preceding 83 years the furthest the national team had been was France!

They might have been able to cope with a quick trip over the English Channel but Wales have not proved to be the greatest of touring sides.

Their record in the southern hemisphere is, to be quite frank, abysmal. Of the big three nations they have only beaten Australia away from home. Twice Wales have managed the feat, 19-16 in Sydney and 22-21 at neutral Rotorua in New Zealand.

But going Down Under to tackle South Africa and New Zealand has proved too

tall an order, even for Welsh sides which had won top honours in Europe.

Wales' first overseas expedition was to Kenya and South Africa in 1964. King's Park, Durban was the venue for the inaugural Test on foreign soil of the joint holders of the Five Nations Championship.

It was an adventure which attracted big crowds in both countries with people anxious to see Wales in the flesh for the first time. The tourists played five matches during the tour. Kenya isn't on the list of destinations for top-ranked rugby countries nowadays but it played host to a number of teams in the past.

Wales' first stop as they headed for the rugby hotbed that is South Africa was

ABOVE Wales' Denzel
Williams (C) feeds
scrum half Clive
Rowlands (Far R)

Nairobi and a clash with East Africa, which they won 26-8.

It was a loosener for the tougher opposition that awaited them. When they moved on to the Republic, Boland were accounted for 17-6 in Wellington. Then came the real tests of Welsh mettle: Northern Transvaal and Orange Free State in the union heartlands.

The first lesson was dished out by Northern as they roared to a 22-9 triumph which sent the locals wild with joy in Pretoria. Wales showed they were keen students by quickly regrouping to beat Free State 14-6 in Bloemfontein.

Of course, they were appetisers for the main fare, the head-to-head with the formidable Springboks at the

famous King's Park. Wales had a strong side captained by the legendary Clive Rowlands, who has filled virtually every major role during a lifetime of service to Welsh rugby.

David Watkins, the first man to captain the British Lions and the Great Britain rugby league team, partnered him at half-back with the visionary John Dawes at centre and Dewi Bebb at left-wing.

Up front, Norman Gale was at hooker, the giant Denzil Williams, a forerunner of modern-day props like England man-mountain Andrew Sheridan, packed down alongside him while the highly respected pairing of Brian Price and Brian Thomas were at lock forward. Alun Pask, the original free-running back-rower, was at blindside flanker.

But still they weren't good enough, crashing to a crushing 24-3 defeat. It was Wales' heaviest loss for 40 years as they failed to cope with the ferocity and speed of the Springboks' assault in the withering heat. To their credit, Wales earned respect by hanging in there for an hour. But they were unable to prevent the floodgates opening in the final quarter as South Africa ran them ragged.

It was their sixth consecutive reverse against the Springboks and the most comprehensive setback since the 35-10 thumping they endured against Scotland at Inverleith in 1924.

Remarkably, the scoreline at Durban was 3-3 at half-time, thanks to a penalty from Bridgend centre Keith Bradshaw. But negative Wales were guilty of kicking away precious possession, putting themselves under enormous pressure when South Africa ran the ball back at them with purpose.

Although Wales competed strongly at scrummage and line-out, they were unable to match the speed of the nimble home pack around the park. The Dragons were out on their feet towards the end as the rampant Springboks pummelled them with 13 points during a devastating eight-minute spell.

Wales' next overseas adventure occurred four years later, in 1968, when they visited South America and the Latin rugby hotbed of Argentina for two uncapped internationals. Eleven leading players didn't embark on the mission because they were otherwise engaged with the British Lions in South Africa.

Dawes was skipper and the only capped back in the party that faced the Pumas in two matches in Buenos Aires. But there were appearances for future world greats JPR Williams and Phil Bennett. Wales took 13 forwards who had already played international rugby but they struggled to cope with the extra beef and strength of the Argentine pack.

The Pumas won the first Test 9-5 after giving a Welsh eight which contained legendary flanker Dai Morris and John Lloyd a troublesome afternoon. Dawes' side were unable to match the ferocity and willingness of their hot-headed opponents to go in with apparent disregard for their safety.

LEFT Wales' Dewi Bebb (C) breaks a tackle from England's Simon Clarke (L) as England's Peter Jackson (R) looks on

Ebbw Vale scrum-half Glyn Turner, who loved to make sniping runs, got the Welsh try, which Dawes converted.

Argentina's game-plan, as it is today, was based on forward power and a hefty scrummage. They pushed the Wales scrum back in the second clash and jumped for joy after being awarded a pushover try. Jorge Seaton also kicked two penalties. Wales had been six points up thanks to two penalties from Swansea winger Stuart Ferguson, who later added a corner try to ensure a 9-9 draw. That result allowed Wales to return home with some pride still intact. They were not the only team to find out Argentina are formidable opponents, particularly on their own patch, where they have built an impressive record over the years.

New Zealand, South Africa and Australia continued to be frequent visitors to Wales but it was the first appearance of Fiji at Cardiff Arms Park in 1964 that provoked huge interest. There was the novelty factor: the Welsh public had heard of the dazzling skills of the South Pacific islanders and were curious to find out what all the fuss was about.

A crowd of 50,000 showed up and were privileged to witness one of the most compelling and entertaining Tests in history. Wales took on Fiji at their high-speed running game and won a 13-try thriller 28-22, touching down seven times to their opponents' six.

Wales had led 28-9 against a Fiji side reduced to 14 men through injury, but

were holding on for their lives at the end as they ran out of puff. Fiji kept coming at them and scored 13 points in the final 12 minutes to send the pulses of nervous Welsh fans soaring. It was total rugby with visiting prop Sevaro Walisoliso galloping like a back to claim three tries.

Dangerous winger Dewi Bebb, and Aberavon centre Dave Thomas each bagged a brace of touchdowns with Pask, who possessed Fiji-like skills and would have slotted into the islanders' team with ease, Swansea winger David Weaver and Bridgend back-rower Gary Prothero joining them on the scoresheet. Llanelli full-back Terry Price converted two and David Watkins slotted a penalty.

The flamboyant and intensely likeable Clem Thomas, later to become rugby correspondent of *The Observer* newspaper, was captain when Wales hosted Australia in 1958. There was also

the appearance of Carwyn James. He made his debut in the famous No.10 jersey after Cliff Morgan withdrew through injury. James only made one more appearance for his country, at centre later that season as they suffered their first home defeat against France.

His international playing career never took off but James became one of rugby's most influential coaches of all time. He masterminded the Lions' historic Test series triumph over the All Blacks in New Zealand in 1971 and his beloved Llanelli's amazing success against the same opponents at an emotion-charged Stradey Park the following year.

James and Wales struggled in the Arms Park mud to overcome Australia, who weren't a world force at that time. The Wallabies led 3-0 at the interval through a try from Tony Miller and might have been further ahead if they had capitalised on a few telling breaks from Arthur Summons.

Wales responded by going up a gear at forward and keeping the ball 'in-house' in an effort to wear down the Wallabies. An Aussie offence at a scrum was punished by Llanelli full-back Terry Davies and Aberavon wing John Collins was worked over for a corner-try. James added a dropped goal to inflict yet another defeat on the tourists. Australia lost every Test during the tour, suffering 15 defeats in all matches.

The forward-orientated game-plan which had carried Wales to that victory failed to gain them a first victory over South Africa when they clashed in Cardiff in 1960. It wasn't just muddy on this occasion, a fierce gale also blew icy rain across the Arms Park and players were close to suffering from hypothermia when time was eventually called.

There was so much mud it was almost impossible for Scottish referee Jack Taylor to distinguish between the sides. He asked Welsh captain Davies and legendary Springboks skipper Avril Malan whether they wanted the match abandoned with 15 minutes remaining.

But Wales, who trailed 3-0 and had the elements behind them, could scent victory and Davies insisted on the game continuing. Cardiff lock Danny Harris crashed over the try-line from a line-out but Taylor disallowed his alleged score while Bridgend pivot Ken Richards was narrowly wide with a dropped goal.

South Africa adapted to the miserable conditions the better with their forwards driving Wales back and dominating possession. Their tackling was relentless as they protected the lead established through Keith Oxlee's first-half penalty.

New Zealand had never been victorious at the Arms Park, going down in 1905, 1935 and 1953, and were determined to rectify that record when they ran out at the famous Cardiff venue in December 1963. And they had a dangerous weapon in the howitzer

RIGHT New Zealand legend Colin Meads

BELOW Don Clarke, full-back with the New Zealand All Blacks, on a tour of England

boot of full-back Don Clarke.

He had been a major difference between the All Blacks and the Lions during their 1959 Test series. His six penalties at Dunedin had proved vital in beating what many regarded as a superior Lions team 18-17. His radar was slightly off against Wales as he struck the uprights with two massive penalties, one from half-way and the other from an incredible 60 metres.

But Clarke landed an easier effort and outside-half Bruce Watt put the result beyond doubt with a second-half dropped goal. It was a sign of what was to come in future matches between the countries as they held Wales in a stranglehold at forward. The margin could have been greater but the All Blacks were conservative in their approach.

They had already disposed of England, Ireland and France, and drawn with Scotland. Their only defeat of a memorable tour occurred in

Wales, at Rodney Parade when a dropped goal from John Uzzell gave Newport a wonderful 3-0 victory.

The All Blacks captain was Wilson Whineray while they possessed a lock by the name of Colin 'Pinetree' Meads, who remains the best-known Kiwi forward of all time. If there is such a thing as a living legend, it would be the giant from King Country.

Australia returned to Wales in 1966 to face a Dragons side that was in a purple patch with two outright Six Nations crowns and a share of the championship in preceding seasons. The Wallabies had never beaten Wales and weren't expected to be good enough to record a first success. But they defied the odds and capitalised on a below-par Welsh performance to triumph 14-11 in front of 50,000 spectators.

Wales had a habit of under-performing during their autumn internationals and this was another of those occasions. Barry John made his debut at outside-half while there were also first appearances for lock rock Delme Thomas, who led Llanelli to victory over the All Blacks six years later, and the finest Welsh winger of all time, a certain Gerald Davies.

Dawes, Price, Stuart Watkins, Bebb, Denzil Williams, Gale, Lloyd, Price, Pask and Haydn Morgan were all in the Welsh team but they failed to take their opportunities during a wonderful advert for running rugby. Australia, who were captained by scrum-half great Ken Catchpole, overturned an early try from Abertillery and Lions flanker Morgan, through a dropped goal from outside-half Phil Hawthorne.

Full-backs Jim Lenehan and Price exchanged penalties before the former crossed in the corner. Wing Alan Cardy followed him over for the decisive touchdown, Hawthorne converting. Wales replied with a late effort from Davies, Price adding the extra points, but they couldn't pull victory out of the bag. Australia team manager Bill McLaughlin was in tears at the final whistle. They had found the formula to crack Wales and went on to win 12 of their next 18 meetings with the Dragons.

The top crowd draw of the southern hemisphere big three, New Zealand, were back the following year, as they made a short tour that saw them beat England, France, Scotland and Wales.

BELOW Wales team group: (Back row, L-R) Gordon Wells, Ray Prosser, Rhys Williams, John Faull, Roddy Evans, Don Devereux, Haydn Morgan; (Middle row, L-R) Lloyd Williams, Cyril Davies, Malcolm Thomas, Clem Thomas, John Collins, Terry Davies; (Front row, L-R) Bryn Meredith, Cliff Morgan

The comfortable 13-6 success posted by Brian Lochore's side at a wet Arms

ABOVE Wales captain Brian Price leads his team out

RIGHT Wales' Norman Gale (Arms extended C) feeds the ball to his backs, watched by teammates Gary Prothero (L), Alun Pask (Third L), Bill Morris (Fourth R), CH Norris (Third R) and Stuart Watkins (R)

Newport wing forward John Jeffery following an off-target penalty from McCormick allowed inside-centre Bill Davis to pounce for the try which gave the Kiwis an unassailable lead. Skipper Gale landed a penalty but, with Keith Jarrett injured, they lacked a goal-kicker of McCormick's ilk.

On the Five Nations front, Wales were pretty successful between 1954-68 with three outright championships, in 1956, '65 and '66. There were also shared championships, in '54 with England and France, '55 with France and '64 with Scotland.

France had established themselves as a true world force and had the best record during the period with seven titles. Wales came next with six, one more than England. Scotland potted one while poor Ireland had nothing to shout about.

There was just one Welsh Triple Crown, in '65. Stuart Watkins (two) and Morgan got the tries, debut-maker Price converting one and David Watkins putting over a dropped goal, in the 14-3 victory over England at the Arms Park.

Gale powered over for the winning try in a 14-12 success over Scotland at

Park allowed them to square their series with Wales 3-3. Since then they have forged ahead, winning the next 16 encounters with Wales remaining stranded on three.

Full-back Fergie McCormick's penalty and conversion of right-wing Bill Birtwistle's try had fired the All Blacks into an eight-point lead at the interval. John, who had joined Cardiff from Llanelli, gave Wales hope with a dropped goal but a blunder from

Murrayfield. Price converted Stuart Watkins' score and found the target with two crucial penalties. David Watkins and Bebb crossed, Price converting one, kicking a penalty and landing a dropped goal as Ireland were beaten 14-8 in the Triple Crown clincher in Cardiff. It was Wales' 10th Triple Crown as canny captain Clive Rowlands' reign approached its end.

They were already outright champions when they crossed the English Channel but suffered their then heaviest defeat against France. The French stormed into a 22-point advantage before Wales awoke from their slumber, replying with tries from Dawes, Stuart Watkins and Bebb, Price twice converting.

Rowlands' tactics at Murrayfield in 1963 had prompted the banning of kicking directly into touch from outside the 22. He kicked almost every time he received the ball and there was a staggering 111 line-outs as Wales won a boring encounter 6-0.

Chapter 7

1969-79

Television Brings Worldwide Fame

GARETH, BARRY, GERALD, JPR, JJ, 'Merv the Swerve', Benny and the Pontypool front-row, their names reeled off the tongues of the Welsh population as they achieved something no other Welsh side had managed: worldwide fame.

It wasn't just down to the brilliance of the aforementioned Gareth Edwards, Barry John, Gerald and Mervyn Davies, JPR and JJ Williams, Phil Bennett, and the Pooler trio of Graham Price, Bobby Windsor and Charlie Faulkner. There was another factor, which has often been overlooked, for the 1970s heralded the full-scale arrival of colour television.

That meant the glorious exploits of Wales were beamed into homes from Cardiff in the south to Bangor in the north, Brecon in Mid Wales to Fishguard in the west. Seeing their heroes running out for battle wearing the famous red jersey had a profound effect.

Previously, the majority of the public had to watch on black and white screens. It was often difficult to tell who was playing with the kits of Wales, Scotland and Ireland looking virtually the same. If it was muddy, it was hard to identify players. But the advent of the colour tube cleared up the picture and people flocked to sets in droves.

The age of television had really begun and the likes of Edwards, Gerald and JPR almost came leaping out of the screen with their amazing exploits.

Scrum-half wizard Gareth's amazing near length-of-the-field against Scotland at Cardiff Arms Park in 1972 was captured in all its brilliance by the cameras. He probed the blindside of a scrum inside his 22 and accelerated past Rodger Arneil. Edwards, a former athlete and a top gymnast with exceptional power, sprinted clear.

Only Arthur Brown stood between him and the try-line but the close proximity of the touch-line was a concern so Edwards expertly chipped the Scottish full-back and hacked the ball on into the scoring zone. Tartan centre Jim Renwick was racing across to cover but 'Gareth the Great' beat him to the ball, sliding through the mud for

ABOVE Bobby Windsor of the British Lions kicks the ball upfield during the match between Bay of Plenty and the British Lions on 9 August 1977 in Rotorua, New Zealand. The British Lions won the match 23 - 16

what is widely acknowledged as one of the finest individual tries in the history of union.

When he regained his feet, Edwards was coated from head-to-toe in rust-coloured mud. Only his eyes pierced the 'extra layer of skin' he had suddenly acquired until physiotherapist Gerry Lewis towelled his face down to jubilant roars from a crowd that could scarcely believe what it had just witnessed.

The reaction was the same in Welsh homes. This was colour television and rugby at its best, with millions witnessing the moment as it was replayed around the world.

The impact that try, and the one he scored against New Zealand for the Barbarians, when he was on the end of a breathtaking movement, was to have on the psyche of the British and Irish public should not be underestimated.

Until the arrival of colour television, rugby union was regarded as an obscure sport by many in England, Scotland and Ireland, the chasing of an odd-shaped ball by a load of toffs, because it was a middle and upper class game in those countries. Not in Wales, of course, where the 15-a-side code was loved by the masses.

Industrial Wales, with its giant steel plants and coal mines dotted on the landscape of South Wales, needed heroes and Edwards led the way with 20 tries in 53 appearances.

He remains widely acknowledged as the best player in the sport's history, not only through his performances for Wales but also through those for the British and Irish Lions. He and the Welsh influence were pivotal during Test series triumphs in New Zealand in 1971 – still the only one in the land of the long white cloud – and South Africa in 1974.

Youngsters in those countries like Sean Fitzpatrick, the Kiwi who became perhaps the greatest captain of the lot, were

LEFT Wales' Gareth Edwards kicks for touch

inspired. When he messed around with a ball in his garden, Fitzpatrick dreamed of being Edwards.

It wasn't a one-man show, of course, because Wales were blessed with good fortune in that a pool of supreme talent emerged at virtually the same time. To be successful at a sport like rugby and

Alun Pask,
Wales and British Lions

soccer, approximately nearly two-thirds of the team have to be world-class. England possessed that nucleus when they won the 2003 World Cup by beating hosts Australia in Sydney, while Brazil have regularly managed it in soccer.

Picking a weak link in the Wales team of the '70s was mighty difficult. The hard-core of JPR, Gerald, JJ, Barry or Benny, Edwards, Windsor and Merv were there for much of it. Others came and went but most of them had one thing in common: they were formidable operators who would make most line-ups.

Titles, Triple Crowns and Grand Slams piled up. The first championship came in 1969, when Wales were only denied a Grand Slam by an 8-8 draw in Paris with France. Edwards scored a try while his visionary cross-field kick put Maurice Richards in for the other.

Wing Richards could have become a union legend but his record-equalling four tries in his very next game for Wales, the 30-9 humiliation of England in Cardiff, brought him a reputation as one of the best finishers in the world and a prized target for rugby league clubs. The bids rolled in and it wasn't long before he couldn't resist the temptation to head north. Wales' loss

LEFT The Welsh rugby team, 1970. (Back row L-R) Coach Clive Rowlands, D.Thomas, Stuart Gallacher, Barry Llewelyn, Mervyn Davies, Ron Matthias, Dave Morris, John Lloyd and Jack Young. (Seated middle row L-R) Gareth Edwards, John Taylor, John Dawes (capt), John Williams, Arthur Lewis. (Front row) Phil Bennett (L) and Jim Shanklin (R)

TELEVISION BRINGS WORLDWIDE FAME

RIGHT Clive Rowlands kicking the ball in 1966

was the 13-a-side code's gain.

The stunning success against the hapless English brought only Wales' second Triple Crown in 17 years. But it also signalled the start of what has become known as the third Golden Era, a period of unprecedented success that provoked an explosion of interest in union, in countries as far-flung as Australia, Argentina, the United States, Italy and Romania.

Wales were crowned outright European kings in 1969, '71, '75, '76, '78 and '79. They shared it with France in 1970, there was a five-way tie in '73 and no winner in '72 because of the troubles in Ireland. France were winners in 1977 and Ireland three years earlier. Otherwise, it was Wales, Wales...

There were three Grand Slams ('71, '76 and '78) and six Triple Crowns ('69, '71, '76, '77, '78 and '79). Seven championships in 11 years - it could have been eight if it had not been for security problems the other side of the Irish Sea - was a staggering achievement for a country with such a small population.

It was good fortune to have a generation of such talent but Wales were also ahead of the opposition in other areas, like organisation and coaching. Wales' first coach was former international back-row forward David Nash. He served between 1968-69.

That remarkable figure, Clive Rowlands, took over from him. Such was his popularity that he had been elected as a vice-president of the Welsh Rugby Union less than two months after retiring from playing in April 1968.

Wales also had a coaching organiser

of note in Ray Williams, who later became secretary of the WRU. It was he who went to Australia and encouraged the Wallabies to put a system in place which resulted in them becoming the first country to win two World Cups.

The Welsh were ahead of the game, so to speak. Weekend training sessions were introduced for the national squad at Afan Lido, Port Talbot with workouts often taking place on Aberavon beach. Clubs were asked not to play their

BELOW Gerald Davies of the British Lions in action during the British Lions Tour to New Zealand in 1971

international stars in more than one match a week.

Back then, most clubs also played midweek. Seasons were shorter but contained more fixtures although it didn't have the same intensity as today because the advent of professionalism has resulted in training programmes, and bigger, fitter, faster and more powerful players.

Rather like the Welsh team of today, it took

Edwards and company time to acquire the winning habit. John, who was crowned 'King Barry' after steering the Lions to series glory in New Zealand in 1971, had made his Wales debut in the 1966 victory over Australia.

Edwards arrived on the international scene a few months later but it wasn't until they lined up at half-back against New Zealand in November 1967 that the supreme commanders - John, by that stage, had left Llanelli for Cardiff and the pair were club-mates - were flung together at the highest level.

Wales showed promise but it took time and patience before they began fulfilling their potential. But, come 1969, they began to blossom with their biggest victory over Scotland at Murrayfield since 1947. It was not a coincidence that this match heralded the debuts of JPR and Merv, two more who were to have a profound influence.

Merv was one of the great No.8 forwards. A beanpole he might have been but he was an audaciously talented footballer and a hard man. He also proved to be a great captain, leading

Wales to back-to-back Grand Slams.

His aim was three in a row but fate conspired against him and nearly cost 'Swerve' his life, when he suffered a brain haemorrhage during a Schweppes Cup semi-final between his club Swansea and Pontypool in 1976. Davies was stretchered off but, thankfully, survived major surgery. He never played again but remains highly regarded for his astute and forthright analysis of the sport.

John, Edwards and Richards crossed against Scotland in 1969 while Keith Jarrett, now playing at centre, converted one and landed two penalties. Jarrett's is a fascinating story, particularly his amazing debut two seasons earlier.

He had only left Monmouth School four months before being selected by his country. Jarrett had made a mark at centre with Newport but the national selectors picked him out of position at full-back against England at the Arms Park.

A trial run for the Black and Ambers against Newbridge in his unaccustomed position didn't go well and there were fears he would be out of his depth when the big day came.

He scored a spectacular try when he latched on to an England clearance and counter-attacked from his half. Jarrett kept running and running and ended up touching down in the corner. It was a fairytale debut as he converted all five tries and put over two penalties during a record-breaking 34-21 triumph.

Jarrett's quickly-taken tapped penalty in 1969 put Wales on the road to denting Ireland's Triple Crown bid in Cardiff, and they romped to a 29-11 success.

BELOW Keith Jarrett

they had a right trouncing against the All Blacks although, it must be said, the demanding schedule didn't help their chances, with three Tests in seven games and the opening match of the trip coming just four days after a 52-hour journey.

No-nonsense New Zealand had too many weapons at forward and blitzed Wales 19-0 in Christchurch and 33-

ABOVE Wales' Dai Morris (Centre L) and Scotland's Gordon Brown (Centre R) fail to reach the ball at a line out

RIGHT Wales's John Taylor (L) beats New Zealand's Sid Going (R) to the ball following a long kick downfield

Like, Richards and David Watkins, the first man to skipper Britain at union and league, Jarrett was lost to raiders from the north of England.

Wales went to the southern hemisphere as Five Nations kings for a daunting tour of New Zealand, Australia and Fiji. And

12 in Auckland, with full-back Fergie McCormick setting a then world record with 24 points at Eden Park. Richards scored another gem, but it became a learning exercise for Rowlands' men.

Wales trailed 11-0 against Australia in Sydney but hit back with tries from the 'Shadow', flanker Dai Morris, Gerald Davies and John Taylor to edge a thriller 19-16. Davies was in the process of being converted from centre to wing and was to become a colossus.

Fiji were beaten 31-11 in Suva and there was confidence Wales could beat South Africa for the first time. Results during their tour of Britain and Ireland showed it was one of the poorest Springbok sides but still Wales couldn't get the better of them, only a late try from master poacher Edwards giving them a fortunate 6-6 draw.

The Welsh selectors were so keen to have Llanelli maestro Bennett in the team that they made room for him. Bennett was the first man to win a cap as a Wales replacement and made his first start at wing against South Africa.

He was at centre when they opened the 1970 Five Nations Championship with an 18-9 home victory over Scotland and also appeared as a replacement full-back when JPR was injured. But outside-half was his rightful position and he prospered after John's shock retirement in 1972.

Bennett went on to captain the 1977 Lions in New Zealand and led his country

ABOVE Graham Price of the British Lions pictured during the Second Test match between New Zealand and the British Lions on 9 July 1977 in Christchurch, New Zealand. The British Lions won the match 13 - 9

to a famous Grand Slam the following year, scoring two brilliant tries and inspiring Wales to a narrow triumph in the gripping, winner-take-all decider with France at the Arms Park.

It was the brilliant sidestepping magician's final Test appearance. He bowed out having become the championship's then record points-scorer with a total haul of 166.

The 1978 team was hailed as one of the greatest of all time by coach John Dawes, who knew all about leadership having skippered the Lions to success in New Zealand seven years earlier.

Wales fielded six new caps - Steve Fenwick, Ray Gravell, John Bevan, Faulkner, Price and Trevor Evans - in Paris in 1975 and still won, 25-10. Price's amazing try, for a prop, put the icing on a sublime performance.

There were individual moments to savour during the decade, like the

wonderful touchline conversion from Taylor of Gerald Davies' try that allowed Wales to sneak a last-ditch 19-18 victory over Scotland at Murrayfield in 1971. Then there was the world record crowd of 104,000 at the same venue in 1975. On that occasion 40,000 Welshmen and women made the journey north only to see Wales flop 12-10 and Bennett have an awful afternoon.

But he redeemed himself during his

next visit to Scotland, two years later, when rounding off a brilliant team try instigated by the superbly balanced Gerald. JPR couldn't stop scoring tries against England and never lost against them in 10 outings.

Although Wales were acclaimed as European kings they couldn't beat New Zealand - apartheid in South Africa meant they didn't face the Springboks for 24 years - despite providing the nucleus of the winning 1971 and 1974 Lions.

The All Blacks won 19-16 thanks to the accurate goal-kicking of Joe Karam in 1972 in Cardiff, JPR's 'alleged' try being disallowed for a supposed double-movement. If that defeat was adjudged harsh, there was heartbreak in 1978 when Kiwi locks Andy Haden and Frank Oliver dived out of a line-out soccer-style and won a penalty which replacement Brian McKechnie, also

a Test cricketer, put over to give them a fortunate and highly contentious 13-12 success. Haden later admitted it had been pre-planned.

Not beating New Zealand was about the only real blot on Wales' copybook. They accounted for Australia 24-0 in 1973 and 28-3 two years later, both at the Arms Park.

However, without Edwards and Bennett, they failed to win either Test in Australia in the summer of 1978. Wales were mugged amid allegations of biased refereeing and violent tactics by the Wallabies with Price having his jaw broken by a sneak off-the-ball punch from Steve Finane.

But with new stars like battering ram scrum-half Terry Holmes and outside-half Gareth Davies, they recovered from that ordeal and from being robbed by New Zealand, to win the 1979 Five Nations title and their fifth Triple Crown of the decade. Normal business had seemingly resumed. Little did they know, it wasn't to last indefinitely.

ABOVE John Dawes leads his team out at Cardiff Arms Park

LEFT J.P.R. Williams of Wales one of the legends of rugby in action for Wales in the game against Australia in 1978

Chapter 8

1980-89
Bitter
Disappointment

WHILE THE 1970s HAD BROUGHT unrivalled success and joy, the following decade proved to be a bitter disappointment. It was an anti-climax as rugby's growing profile brought pressure which, for a time, stifled flair.

There was so much riding on results that teams often resorted to violence. Punch-ups punctuated the early 1980s, until touch judges were given the power to bring referees' attention to foul play.

It was a start to cleaning up the sport and an increase in the number of television cameras at matches meant that virtually every angle was soon covered. The role of the hit-man was to lessen.

Wales' dominance of European rugby could be seen by the make-up of British and Irish Lions touring parties. Fourteen Welsh stars went to Australia and New Zealand in 1971, nine to South Africa in 1974, an incredible 18 to New Zealand and Fiji in 1977 and, in a knock-on effect of the Golden Era, 15 made the trip to South Africa in 1980.

The latter contingent included veterans Allan Martin, Ray Gravell and Derek Quinnell while there were bright young things like the redoubtable Terry Holmes, a fierce competitor and one of the most committed and certainly, the strongest scrum-half to represent Wales and the Lions, Gareth Davies and silky centre David Richards.

However, analysis of subsequent Lions tours highlights the decline of

Clive Woodward (Centre) of England passes the ball to a team mate whilst being tackled by Welsh scrum half Terry Holmes during the Five Nations Championship match at Cardiff Arms Park, 1985. Wales won the match 24-15

Wales during the '80s. Just eight went to New Zealand in 1983, and the same number were on the winning tour of Australia in 1989.

Wales also came under renewed attack from rugby league during the decade. Because results weren't so good, players were more likely to succumb to temptation and big money offers from the likes of Widnes, Leeds and Warrington.

During the super '70s, the stars had been reluctant to leave their homeland. Who could blame them when the team was setting the standard and they were fêted as heroes?

The '80s were a different kettle of fish. Holmes and giant prop Stuart Evans

BITTER DISAPPOINTMENT

were the pioneers while mercurial outside-half Jonathan Davies sparked a mass exodus following the 'tour of death' to New Zealand in 1988, when Wales were humiliated by one of the best teams in history.

John Devereux, Adrian Hadley, David Young, Rowland Phillips, Paul Moriarty, Jonathan Griffiths and Mark Jones were among those that followed. It was a tragedy for Welsh rugby because the team that surprised the rugby world by

finishing third at the inaugural World Cup, in Australia and New Zealand in 1987, possessed vast potential.

They had gone to New Zealand the following year as Triple Crown winners and joint Six Nations champions with France after being pipped by Les Bleus as they chased a Grand Slam in their final match of the European campaign.

Wales had, thankfully, reverted to running rugby but the pouring rain that fell on Cardiff Arms Park didn't help their cause. Half-backs Robert Jones and Davies struggled in the wet and muddy conditions and chances went begging during the first half.

France, World Cup finalists the previous year, started slowly and looked unsure of themselves. But their confidence grew as Wales failed to punish them and it sunk in it that wasn't the forlorn mission the French had feared.

Deadly finisher Ieuan Evans scored the Welsh try, full-back Paul Thorburn converting and kicking a penalty. But Les Bleus sneaked it 10-9, thanks to a try

ABOVE Wales star John Devereux (L) of Wales, catches the ball during the Rugby World Cup semi-final between New Zealand and Wales in Brisbane, Australia. New Zealand triumphed 49-6, 1987

LEFT Robert Jones (Centre right) the ball during the Rugby World Cup third-place play-off between Wales and Australia in Rotorua, New Zealand. Wales edged it 22-21, 1987

from giant outside-half Jean-Patrick Lescarboura and two penalties from extravagant winger Jean-Baptiste Lafond.

The pair were hailed as super-subs by French fans. Dax play-maker Lescarboura had only been called in when points-machine Didier Camberabero dropped out, while Racing Club star Lafond had taken over from Philippe Berot who withdrew suffering from injury.

Rain lashed down on the dejected Welsh fans as they trooped away from the Arms Park knowing a golden opportunity had passed their team of young guns. It was a disappointing end to an otherwise memorable Five Nations campaign.

Wales had been building for a couple of years and had a new talisman in the gifted Davies. He was to prove one of the great attacking outside-halves, possessing

MIDDLE Richie Collins of the Wales Rugby Union Team during a squad photocall before their match against Fiji on their tour of Tonga Fiji and Samoa, 1994

RIGHT Welsh players including Robert Jones and No.15 Paul Thorburn celebrate after Jonathan Davies scores a drop goal during the Five Nations Championship match against Scotland at Cardiff Arms Park in Cardiff, Wales, 1988. Wales won the match 25-20

the pace to take on defenders and leave them clutching air.

Before the '88 title race had even kicked off, Wales made their intentions clear by dropping master goal-kicker Thorburn. They went into the match with England at Twickenham without a recognised marksman and a rookie full-back in Anthony Clement.

The Swansea player was an outside-half and had never previously worn the No.15 jersey. It was reminiscent of Keith Jarrett's debut against the English in 1967. Clement didn't score any points but he made a considerable impact.

Wales planned to keep the ball alive and had selected four fly-halves in Davies, the audaciously talented Mark Ring, influential skipper Bleddyn Bowen and Clement. The idea was to run England ragged. Davies jetted past England flanker and hard-hitting tackler Mick 'the Munch' Skinner and looked to be heading for the try-line. But he was brought down inches short by the cover.

However, they kept preservering and

the rewards came later. Clement launched a counter-attack after fielding a miscued tactical kick from Red Rose play-maker Les Cusworth and it culminated in the powerful Hadley going over.

Wales' second try was a gem, with the ball going through a multitude of hands as they went left, right and left again. Davies made a curving run and Ring's dummy opened up the home defence. Forwards Robert Norster and flying flanker Richie Collins, also a basketball international, handled before Hadley came back on an angle and used his strength to bundle Cusworth out of the way. Hadley made a habit of scoring tries against England during his career.

There had been Welsh line-out wobbles early on but the arrival of replacement hooker Ian Watkins for the

ABOVE Adrian Hadley scored both tries when Wales beat England 11-3 at Twickenham in 1988

injured Kevin Phillips had a dramatic impact. The Ebbw Vale star and the athletic Norster immediately hit it off, plucking his first throw out of the air. From that moment on, Wales never looked back.

Even their lack of a goal-kicker didn't matter. Davies put over a trademark dropped goal while England's only points during an 11-3 reverse that stunned Red Rose supporters into silence at Twickenham came from full-back Jonathan Webb, now a leading sports surgeon.

Hamstring trouble kept Clement out of the next match of a memorable campaign, the classic with Scotland at the Arms Park. The dependable Thorburn was recalled at full-back and converted two of Wales' three tries. He also put over a penalty.

Scotland were 7-0 up after five minutes when centre Allan Tait, later to become a team mate of Davies at rugby league club Widnes, put over right-wing Matt Duncan and they led 20-10 at the start of the second-half.

Davies had brought Wales back into it with a magnificent individual try. He attacked from a scrum, put a deft grubber-kick past Scottish No.8 forward Derek White and won the race to the line.

A brilliant three-quarter move gave Evans a glint of an opening and he sidestepped five times off his right foot on a breath-taking run that culminated when he dived over despite the attention of covering prop David Sole. Rugby com-

mentator supreme Bill McLaren gushed, "Merlin the Magician couldn't have done better."

There was still work to be done and Watkins was pushed over by his team mates after Thorburn was collared just short. A dropped goal from Davies put them in front with 10 minutes remaining and he repeated the feat soon afterwards to make it 25-20.

Wales hadn't clinched a Triple Crown for nine years and had failed to win the Five Nations during the decade. Suddenly, it was on, prompting thousands of extra Welsh fans to

LEFT Wales's Paul Moriarty takes on the French during the Rugby League World cup match at Ninian Park, Cardiff

BITTER DISAPPOINTMENT

make last-minute plans to go to Dublin.

As usual, the wind swirled around a cold Lansdowne Road and it was a match that suited the spoiler. Conditions made it difficult to handle the ball and it developed into a war of attrition.

Ireland hooker Terry Kingston had scored after charging down an attempted clearance by Jones while a back-row move had sent No.8 forward Paul Moriarty over for the Welsh try. The kickers, Michael Kiernan and Thorburn, had cancelled each other's efforts out and it was all square going into injury time when Wales were awarded a penalty. Thorburn stepped up and blasted it between the uprights. Ecstatic Welsh fans turned Dublin red that night as they partied into the early hours.

Aside from the setback against France that was to follow, it had been a good year for Wales. They headed Down Under in high spirits, eager for another chance to test themselves against New Zealand.

They had been crushed a record 49-6 by the All Blacks in their World Cup semi-final a year earlier but their comparatively young team had im-proved in the meantime.

However, the world champions had also got better. They were a well-oiled, relentless and ruthless rugby machine, attacking in waves. Wales had been softened up by the Kiwi provinces they had faced and the body count was huge with a host of casualties being sent home early.

Norster skippered Wales for the first time but suffered a nasty gash from a ferocious rucking and was forced out of the second Test. Wingers John Kirwan (four) and Terry Wright (two) got six of New Zealand's 10 tries during a record

BITTER DISAPPOINTMENT

tries but goal-kicker Grant Fox was imperious, converting the lot and adding two penalties during a 54-9 hammering. The series was summed up by Mason's ripped jersey. It was practically hanging from his back after he took a real rucking. The Pontypridd star wasn't the only victim as New Zealand bullied Wales out of their way with their aggression.

Wales had been defeated in six of their eight matches and emergency action was called for. Davies pleaded to be allowed to address the annual general meeting of the Welsh Rugby Union about the direction it needed to take if Wales were to match New Zealand, who were professional in all but name, but it refused. Instead, the WRU sacked coach Tony Gray.

The fallout was immense. Soon Davies had jumped ship and it wasn't long before many of his team mates and

52-3 mauling in Christchurch.

Wales scored a consolation try in the second rubber, Ring and replacement full-back Jonathan Mason, who had been summoned from a Greek holiday beach when Clement was injured, combined before sending stand-in captain Davies on a 65m sprint, that brought ironic applause from the Eden Park crowd.

They restricted the All Blacks to eight

friends were also residing in the north of England. Getting paid to take a kicking was much more acceptable. Who could blame them?

But the downside was that Wales lost most of its leading players. What it meant was that the top of its pyramid had all but gone and Welsh rugby supporters never found out how much that team could have developed.

It had pulled off a notable feat at the World Cup the previous year when it bounced back from its semi-final thumping against the All Blacks in Brisbane to beat Australia 22-21 in the third-place play-off at Rotorua, New Zealand.

The Wallabies had flanker David Codey sent off after just four minutes for an outrageous piece of stamping. It was a cliffhanger with the lead changing hands five times. Wales grabbed victory in the fifth minute of injury time when Thorburn put

Hadley in at the corner. Thorburn kept his composure and nailed a magnificent conversion.

Centre Devereux, a student at South Glamorgan Institute of Higher Education (now UWIC), the academy

LEFT Former Welsh rugby star Paul Ringer

BITTER DISAPPOINTMENT

Australia had humiliated Wales 28-9 at Cardiff Arms Park in November 1984. The writing was on the wall almost from the off on that occasion as the Wallabies worked the blindside to feed the legendary David Campese. The winger cut inside and skipper Andy Slack was on hand to put teenager and future star Michael Lynagh over.

Wales even suffered the indignity of conceding a pushover try. And Aussie outside-half Mark Ella, who was to cross in every Test as they completed a first Grand Slam against the home nations, intercepted a pass from Eddie Butler to stroll to the line to rub more salt into a gaping wound.

Bright spot for Wales was live wire scrum-half David Bishop. He juggled the ball but managed to get full control of it to net their only try. Amazingly, it was his only cap.

There were other significant defeats which had produced an illustrious list of internationals headed by Gareth Edwards, had caused havoc during the tournament with his piston-like hand-off.

during the decade. It had started badly when flanker Paul Ringer was dismissed for a late and head-high tackle on England outside-half John Horton at Twickenham in 1980.

Wales played for 75 minutes a man short and were pipped 9-8 by an England side that went on to win the Grand Slam. It wasn't a surprise somebody was sent off because the tension had been building to a crescendo during the lead-up.

In a sign of things to come, the Dragons were put in their place by New Zealand later that year. The All Blacks romped to a 23-3 defeat, inflicting what was then Wales' heaviest post-war home defeat.

Wales managed to beat Australia 18-13 at the Arms Park. The Wallabies were yet to unearth Campo, Lynagh and a pack of forwards able to compete at the top level.

But a downward spiral was around the corner. Wales' record of 27 Five Nations fixtures in Cardiff without defeat was brought to a shuddering halt by Scotland in March 1982. Nothing went right for them as they conceded a record five tries at home during a 34-18 hammering.

Despite the manful efforts of Holmes, Wales struggled for consistency. Their reputation had diminished to such an extent that Romania were ready, willing and able to ambush them in Bucharest the following year, emerging emphatic 24-6 winners.

Japan also scared the daylights out of Wales. There was another home defeat against Scotland. France also triumphed in Cardiff and England pulled off a draw. An Irish success in 1985 condemned Wales to their fourth loss in a row at the Arms Park. Almost unbelievably, they then failed to beat Ireland in the Welsh capital until the Grand Slam clinching success 20 years later.

There was an embarrassing 15-9 home reverse against Romania. It was Davies' last match before switching to league, a debacle too far. A surprise victory over England in 1989 staved off a Five Nations whitewash but they were again no match for New Zealand, suffering a then record 34-9 defeat in Cardiff.

Thorburn did provide one astonishing moment against Scotland in 1986, when he put over an amazing 70m wind-assisted penalty. Welsh fans were disconsolate but there was more misery on the way.

Chapter 9

1990-98
Dark Days

THE 1980s HAD BEEN A TRYING experience for devoted followers of Welsh rugby but their despair grew deeper the following decade as Wales went through coaches and numerous players at an unprecedented rate.

There were seven coaches between 1990-98, a staggering 98 new caps and four secretaries of the Welsh Rugby Union. The organisation had only five between its founding in 1881 and 1988 but that number doubled in the next 10 years.

Ray Williams was replaced by former South Wales Police chief constable David East in 1989 but his tenure lasted only a matter of months. He resigned in protest at the manner of the recruitment of Welsh players for a World XV to face then pariahs South Africa.

An enormous row culminated with the 230 plus member clubs forcing a Extra-ordinary General Meeting. Committee members were voted off and an inquiry was held.

That fiasco was among many to blight Welsh rugby as it came close to imploding. It lurched from one crisis to another and the WRU was clearly incapable of dealing with the professional era that was rapidly approaching.

The general committee still held the power strings and were reluctant to hand them over to its professional officers. The secretary was at the mercy of the elected members of the committee, a large and unwieldy body.

Denis Evans, a former Wales centre, succeeded the top law enforcer. His reign was colourful and courted in controversy. He famously summoned coaching organiser John Dawes and assistant Malcolm Lewis to his office to

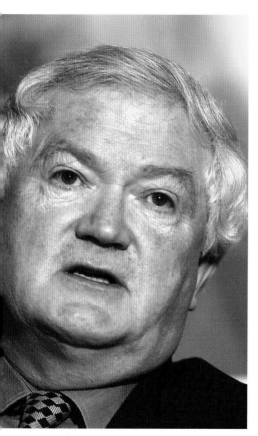

That was Evans's style, blunt and confrontational. He brought in a high profile marketing guru in Jonathan Price and Wales were billed as the Dragons in an attempt to attract more fans as they struggled to fill Cardiff Arms Park for non-Five Nations Championship matches.

But it was a short reign. Evans had frequent spats with the media and, fatally, with the general committee. He took them on in a giant power struggle. It was one he was not to win.

Evans was accused of bullying by WRU treasurer Glanmor Griffiths and suspended from his post. He never returned to it. The committee had won the war and continued to fudge over policy.

An impressive paper, which had been put together by Evans, called the Quest For Excellence, was shelved. Not that it was unusual because it joined

LEFT Glanmor Griffiths, the chairman of the Welsh Rugby Union, masterminded the building of the Millennium Stadium in Cardiff

tell them they were fired. The pair were told to pack their bags and leave.

numerous documents sitting in the WRU offices gathering dust.

Sidekick Price also left the body and Evans's assistant Edward Jones was promoted to secretary. Leading QC Vernon Pugh, who had headed an inquiry into alleged WRU involvement in signing up players for the World XV to face South Africa, filled the vacuum as power shifted from the committee to the new post of honorary chairman.

Pugh was an extremely clever advocate and had a charming way of convincing the general committee to back his ideas. But he was also a visionary and knew professionalism was inevitable.

He was soon sitting on the International Rugby Board, as a WRU representative, and his smooth style, intellect and intelligence quickly had delegates from other countries looking to him for leadership.

The Welsh speaker became chairman of the IRB and announced, in August 1995, it had voted that rugby union become an open game, allowing the payment of players. Professionalism had arrived. Sadly Wales were not ready for it and got left behind.

The rush to sign up players put many clubs in trouble as they failed to adhere to the basic rule of business, that income must exceed outgoings. Players were offered huge salaries as the Welsh clubs competed against the new set-ups across the border, as English rugby, backed by genuine money-men, had its own revolution.

While England moved rapidly to a professional structure, Wales was left in the Dark Ages. Squabbles continued and, eventually, Pugh stood down from the chairman's post in 1997 and as a committee member of the WRU to devote his efforts to being chairman of the IRB.

The affable Jones had preceded him by quitting a year earlier. Richard Jasinski was recruited but the move wasn't a success. He struggled to cope with the petty rows, tribalism and factions that make up Welsh rugby.

It was an unhappy time and he occupied the post for barely a year. The likeable Dennis Gethin, a former local authority chief executive, became the WRU's last secretary, the post being scrapped when the body was reorganised and streamlined in 2002.

There was trouble on and off the field. It was a real fire-fighting exercise just to keep heads above water with rows constantly plastered over the

sports pages of the Welsh newspapers.

Reporting on rugby took a back seat. There were less stories about injuries, team selections and matches, and more on the farcical soap opera that continued unabated.

There was a fresh row virtually every day. The Western Mail had a headline, "Another typical day in Welsh Rugby." Underneath it were reports of three new conflicts that had broken out in a 24-hour period.

Rugby writers were more like parliamentary correspondents as they were called upon to report on the politics of the WRU and Welsh rugby. It was unprecedented and chaotic. The union had lost its grip of the game and lurched from one crisis to another.

A gilt-edged opportunity to get into bed with England and form an Anglo-Welsh League was wasted, not by the union but the top clubs. A formative tournament, held in midweek, took place during the early days of professionalism but the Welsh clubs foolishly entered weakened teams because qualification for the European Cup came from their domestic league and it soon petered out.

It was an enormous and costly mistake

ABOVE Wales replacement Mike Rayer aqua-planes over the line for the first of his two tries during the 29-6 demolition of Scotland in 1994

ing a damaging impact.

There was also another factor: satellite television. The advent of Sky and its live coverage of Premiership rugby in England and the crack southern hemisphere Super 12 tournament meant Welsh subscribers didn't have to leave their homes. They could sit in the comfort of their armchairs and watch vastly superior products for less than the entrance fee at their local club.

Cardiff and Swansea were expelled from the Welsh League by the WRU after announcing a plan to play England's premier clubs in an unofficial, rebel Anglo-Welsh League in 1998. They refused to bow to pressure from the governing body and went ahead.

Initially, it was a great success as teams like Bath, Leicester and Saracens paraded full-strength sides. Matches drew capacity crowds to the Cardiff Arms Park club ground and St. Helen's.

because the only hope club rugby had of coming anywhere near to sustaining itself in Wales and not by having to rely on hand-outs from the WRU, was by a tie-up with England and its potential to attract capacity crowds.

Instead gates plummeted as the public lost interest. Bonus points were introduced - one of the WRU's better initiatives - in an effort to make the sport more attractive, but the conflicts, low skill levels and boring matches were hav-

It showed the potential of an official cross-border league.

England offered a peace deal with entry for five Welsh teams into its league structure. They proposed two in the top tier and three in the First Division with promotion and relegation. But Llanelli, who were earmarked for the lower tier, led the campaign against it and talks broke down.

Cardiff and Swansea, who had been sanctioned by the WRU, didn't have anywhere to go and returned to the Welsh League the following season.

Ironically, although they had been ostracised by the WRU, it never stopped Wales selecting players from Cardiff and Swansea for the national team. Needs prevailed!

Not that it helped much. Wales' only silverware of the decade came during the 1994 Five Nations Championship when winger Ieuan Evans led them to the title.

There were some great players, people like Evans, Robert Jones, Scott Gibbs, Robert Howley, Scott Quinnell and Allan Bateman. And there was a certain Neil Jenkins, who was the subject of endless debate because he wasn't a traditional Welsh running outside-half.

The 'Ginger Monster' became world rugby's highest points-scorer in history with 1,090 during a career that saw him capped 87 times by Wales and make

BELOW Scrum-half Robert Howley kicks from the base of a scrum as Ireland's Gabriel Fulcher attempts to block it during a Five Nations match between Ireland and Wales at Lansdowne Road in 1996

DARK DAYS

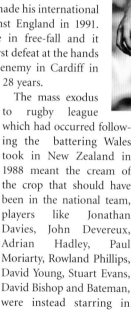

four Test appearances for the British and Irish Lions. Three of them were as a full-back, a position he also filled for Wales, during the Lions tour of South Africa in 1997. His deadly goal-kicking gave the tourists a thrilling 2-1 triumph over the then world champions in a riveting Test series.

Jenkins made his international debut against England in 1991. Wales were in free-fall and it was their first defeat at the hands of the old enemy in Cardiff in 28 years.

The mass exodus to rugby league which had occurred following the battering Wales took in New Zealand in 1988 meant the cream of the crop that should have been in the national team, players like Jonathan Davies, John Devereux, Adrian Hadley, Paul Moriarty, Rowland Phillips, David Young, Stuart Evans, David Bishop and Bateman, were instead starring in the north of England.

League was still picking off Welsh players. Gibbs and Quinnell were among those who were to join Davies and Co. in the 13-a-side heartlands of Lancashire and Yorkshire.

When union went professional in 1995 a number of them returned to the 15-a-side code, joining clubs in England or Wales. But it was too late for Wales because many were approaching the twilight of their careers. A generation had been lost. One wonders how different it might have been had they never headed north.

Wales' first international of the 1990s, against France at the Arms Park, was remembered for the wrong reason: Pontypool lock Kevin Moseley was sent off five minutes before half-time for stamping on wing Marc Andrieu and suspended for 33 weeks.

The seven remaining forwards held on and only trailed by two points with

six minutes remaining. But France bagged two tries to win 29-19. It was their eighth victory in a row over Wales.

Things went downhill, at a considerable rate of knots. Wales were humiliated 34-6 by England at Twickenham. Coach John Ryan, who had taken over from Tony Gray two years earlier, was a man of honour and resigned. He couldn't stomach any more after watching some of the players allegedly waving to their

LEFT English referee Fred Howard sends off Welsh lock Kevin Moseley during the 1990 Five Nations Championship clash with France

DARK DAYS

families in the crowd at half-time.

Neath were Wales' most successful club at that time and their team manager Ron Waldron took over as national coach. Six of his players lined up against Scotland but they were beaten 13-9 in Cardiff.

A 14-8 defeat in Ireland condemned them to a first Five Nations whitewash. Statistics revealed they were the worst Welsh team in history with a record number of points having been conceded.

There were factions in the squad. A number of leading players made themselves unavailable for the tour of Namibia and there were 10 withdrawals from the original selection. Wales won the first Test 18-10 but struggled to a 34-30 success against the minnows in the second.

Waldron opted to include more Neath players the following season against the Barbarians. Nine lined up and Wales were taken to the cleaners at the line-out, losing the match 31-24.

Defeat against England was followed by a 32-12 walloping in Scotland. The prospect of another whitewash was staved off by a 21-21 home draw with Ireland. Wales were caned 36-3 in Paris as France ran riot with rookie Welsh prop John Davies being given 'flying lessons' at the scrum.

Going to Australia that summer was hardly a recipe for recovery and so it proved. Wales conceded 13 tries as they fell to a record defeat in a representative match when they were hammered 71-8 by New South Wales.

They restricted Australia to 63-6 during the Brisbane Test but there were embarrassing and disgraceful scenes afterwards with an argument between Welsh players at the after-match function escalating into a scuffle.

Waldron returned home sick with a blood clot on a lung and stood down. The 1991 World Cup was just three months away and Wales were in their most damaging crisis.

BELOW Llanelli's John Davies celebrates victory after the Heineken Cup quarter-final with Bath at the Recreation Ground

Pragmatic Nottingham coach Alan Davies was appointed caretaker and Wales showed more appetite for battle during a 22-9 World Cup warm-up defeat against France at the Arms Park. It was the first floodlit international at the famous old ground.

But Wales' World Cup challenge evaporated at the first hurdle when they slumped to a shock 16-13 defeat after being battered black and blue by the ferocious tackling of the Western Samoa hard-men.

They recorded their first win in nine attempts by accounting for Argentina 16-7 but had to beat Australia to progress to the quarter-finals. Wales crashed to a record 38-3 home defeat, winning just two out of 30 line-outs.

Davies, though, had impressed with the management structure he put in place, and his role was made permanent. He shored up the defence and made changes to improve the line-out. They beat Ireland 16-15 away, narrowly went down 12-9 to France, restricted powerful England to a 24-point win and defeated Scotland 15-12 in 1992.

Australia again came to Cardiff and conquered but Wales were playing with more organisation and spirit. It was that determination which gave them a shock 10-9 victory over England after Evans had sneaked up on England wing Rory Underwood following a chip from flanker Emyr Lewis.

Elation was followed by dejection as they lost their remaining three matches. There was more misery when they slumped 26-24 to their first defeat against Canada, at the Arms Park in November 1993, a match

which marked Quinnell's debut.

The Canucks were certainly not mugs, having reached the quarter-finals of the 1991 World Cup and having given a good account of themselves against New Zealand. Chunky outside-half Gareth Rees, whose parents were Welsh, sunk Davies' men with the final kick, a conversion of Al Charron's try.

Wales went into the 1994 Five Nations with expectations low but replacement Mike Rayer twice aqua-planed over the try-line as they powered to a confidence-boosting 29-6 triumph over Scotland. Ireland were pipped 17-15 in Dublin while Quinnell and former Olympic

hurdler Nigel Walker were the heroes in the 24-15 victory over France - their first success against Les Bleus since 1982.

England denied them a Grand Slam and Triple Crown with a 15-8 win at Twickenham but Wales won the championship on points difference, which was an innovation introduced by tournament organisers.

The bubble burst the following year. Wales were decimated by injuries and crashed to the Wooden Spoon and a second whitewash. Davies sought a vote of confidence from the general committee but it didn't materialise and he resigned.

Shades of 1991, they didn't have a

DARK DAYS

coach and the World Cup was a matter of months away. Australian Alex Evans, who had done a sterling job with Cardiff, headed a caretaker management team at the World Cup in South Africa. Defeats against New Zealand and Ireland, during a dreadful match, again eliminated them at the pool stage.

Kevin Bowring took over and Wales proceeded to play an exciting brand of rugby but three defeats took their losing streak in the Five Nations to eight. They ended it with a shock 16-15 success over France but were smashed 56-25 and 42-0 in Australia.

There was another false dawn, a 34-19 try-fest in Scotland in 1997, as Gibbs and Bateman showed their class but Wales didn't have enough power at forward and lost against Ireland, France and England. The latter, a 34-13 defeat, was the last international at the Arms Park before it was demolished to make way for the Millennium Stadium.

Wembley became Wales' main temporary accommodation and

they were run off their feet by New Zealand, losing 42-7. A record 60-26 mauling occurred at Twickenham as the low fitness levels of some members of the Welsh team were exposed by ruthless England.

Wales accounted for Scotland and Ireland but the players weren't performing for Bowring and shamefully waved the white flag of surrender against France at Wembley. They hardly made a tackle as they crashed 51-0. It was the end for Bowring.

The ultimate humiliation followed in South Africa when a cross between a second and third team suffered a record 96-13 defeat against the 15-try Springboks in Pretoria. It would have been 100 points but for a dropped pass. It was a new low.

Dennis John was caretaker coach. He came out firing with all guns after the match, vowing to the South Africa media that Wales would beat them within the next year. His startling prediction was to prove accurate.

Chapter 10

1998-2008

Despair, Glory and Disbelief

WALES NEEDED A NEW BROOM after hitting rock-bottom in 1998 and people around the world struggled to comprehend how this once great rugby nation had suffered such a rapid decline in fortunes. The answer lay overseas and the recruitment of a proven coach who would bring real professionalism to Welsh rugby. The hunt was on for the right man and the search led to New Zealand and a former school headmaster named Graham Henry.

Henry had guided the Blues to back-to-back titles against the cream of Australia and South Africa in the Super 12, in 1997 and 1998. It took a lucrative package, worth £1.25 million, to persuade him to sign a five-year deal.

RIGHT Former Auckland Rugby coach Graham Henry gets familarised with a couple of Leeks, the unofficial Welsh national emblem, after a press conference in July 1998 at which he announced he had been appointed Wales coach

Henry was to be paid £250,000 a year, making him the most expensive coach in the world.

Only three of the side swamped by the Springboks – Dafydd James, Mark Taylor and Colin Charvis – remained for the return five months later. It couldn't have worked any better for Henry because it was his first game in charge of Wales and their first since the appalling loss. More than 55,000 people showed up at Wembley for the clash with the world champions.

Centre Taylor made a half-break to put right-wing Gareth Thomas over for a glorious try in the corner. Outside-half Neil Jenkins kicked three penalties and Henry's new charges

were 14 points in front. A shock appeared on the cards. But, against the run of play, South Africa left-wing Peter Rossouw skipped out of an attempted tackle by Jenkins near half-way and put ace poacher Joost van der Westhuizen over for a try. There was also a converted penalty try for a scrum offence but two more Jenkins penalties edged Wales ahead 20-17 with three minutes of normal time remaining.

However, van der Westhuizen burst around the front of a line-out to put flanker Andre Venter for the try which broke Welsh hearts. A final score-line of 28-20 was harsh on Wales.

RIGHT Wales and Lions scrum-half Dwayne Peel makes a break against France in 2005

Welsh fans, eager for success, thought Henry's Wales were the real deal and more than 20,000 embarked on the expedition to Scotland in February 1999. The focus was on Wales but they got off to the worst possible start when Scotland centre John Leslie claimed the kick-off and touched down with just 10 seconds on the clock. Wales battled back and the lead changed five times before Scotland pulled away to win 33-20.

A 29-23 defeat followed for Wales against Ireland during a bad-tempered match at Wembley, opposition hooker Keith Wood side-stepping Scott Gibbs for a gem of a try and Kevin Maggs crossing after a Jenkins clearance was charged down. The bubble which had built up around Henry seemed ready to burst, with an away match to come against France and facing England at Wembley. Twenty-four years had passed since Wales' last victory in Paris and nobody gave them much hope of triumphing during their first visit to the Stade de France.

France, chasing a third Grand Slam in a row, went ahead but Wales came racing back. Wales ran at the French from everywhere during one of the most exciting matches of modern times. Wales were pegged back to 28-28, led 31-28 and trailed 33-31 before a penalty from Jenkins gave them a memorable triumph.

The clash with England was Wales' last home match at Wembley and the final fixture before the Five Nations became Six with the inclusion of Italy. England were chasing a Grand Slam and a record fifth consecutive Triple Crown.

Wales were just about hanging on at half-time with the boot of Jenkins keeping them in touch. He helped create a blindside try for Shane Howarth just after the interval and they were 31-25 down with minutes remaining. Lock Chris Wyatt won the ball at a four-man line-out. No 8 Scott Quinnell juggled it in midfield and the split-second it took to gain control of the ball were vital in flat-footing the English defence.

Centre Gibbs burst on to Quinnell's short pass and roared past Tim Rodber before side-stepping Matt Perry and Steve Hanley for a memorable score. Jenkins converted to give Wales victory. Even the normally emotionless Henry shed a tear following a finish out of Boys' Own.

The finest victory of Henry's reign, and certainly the most significant, was on June 26, almost a year to the day since Wales had been crushed 96-13 by the Springboks. The match was to open the still under-construction

ABOVE Mark Taylor crosses for Wales during a Six Nations battle with England at Twickenham in 2004

were worthy 29-19 victors. The world champions had been beaten by Wales for the first time in history.

Wales opened the World Cup they were hosting with wins over Argentina and Japan but their 10-match winning run came to an end against old foes Samoa, interceptions proving expensive. They still reached the quarter-finals, going down 24-9 against Australia. There were heavy defeats against France and England in the inaugural Six Nations in 2000 – and the eligibility scandal was to cost Wales the services of New Zealand-born pair Howarth and Sinkinson. Their claim, that they each had a Welsh grandparent, was discovered to be false and acute embarrassment resulted.

Lions places were up for grabs in 2001. Henry had been appointed Lions coach for the tour of Australia, which was a considerable motivation for Wales' opponents. England smashed them 44-15 in Cardiff and Wales drew 28-28 in Scotland.

France were beaten 43-35, during another pulsating encounter in Paris and Italy were accounted for 33-23 in Rome. Ten Welsh players were in the Lions party that was beaten 2-1 by

Millennium Stadium and only 27,500 spectators were permitted but they provided an electric atmosphere. Jenkins was in the middle of a purple patch and landed seven of his eight kicks at goal. He also put Thomas over for a corner touchdown. Taylor had bagged the opening try at the ground and Wales

Australia but that trip spelt the beginning of the end for Henry.

Record 36-6 and 54-10 Welsh defeats against Ireland persuaded a mentally exhausted Henry to resign. Fellow Kiwi Steve Hansen took over and only a 44-20 success over Italy prevented a championship rout. There were back to back defeats in South Africa and 2003 saw Wales become the first country to be whitewashed in the Six Nations. A record 11 matches in a row were lost, Hansen's job only being saved by a 23-9 win over Scotland in a World Cup warm-up.

Wales struggled through their group in the world showpiece, narrowly beating Tonga and Italy, but had already qualified for the quarter-finals when they faced New Zealand. With the pressure off, they gave it a go after conceding an early try, eventually losing a marvellous encounter 53-37 in Sydney. Counter-attacks sparked by tricky winger Shane Williams gave Wales new confidence and they burst out of the blocks against England in their Brisbane quarter-final but England's forward power, backed by the accurate tactical kicking of replacement centre Mike Catt, condemned Wales to a 28-17 defeat.

There had been a revolution off the field in Wales with the professional tier, after years of talk, being reduced from nine to five with regional teams Cardiff Blues, Celtic Warriors, Llanelli Scarlets, Newport Gwent Dragons and Neath-Swansea Ospreys being introduced. A year later the Warriors were wound up. At international level, Wales started 2004 brightly with victory over Scotland but could only muster one more success, against Italy. Hansen departed to become Henry's assistant with New Zealand.

Mike Ruddock, who had not applied, finally got the job of national coach when he was parachuted in at the last minute after the WRU decided not to offer the job to the three candidates on its short-list. He shored up the suspect Welsh scrum and line-out and confidence soared following unfortunate 38-26 and 26-25 losses at home to the Springboks and New Zealand. It was critical to capitalise on the feel-

ABOVE Mike Ruddock together with Adam Jones and Mefin Davies raise the trophy as Wales win the Grand Slam in 2005

had grabbed the attention of the world's rugby media with the penalty and his 'rag-doll' tackles on England youngster Mathew Tait.

Wales followed it up with a 38-8 drubbing of Italy in Rome but were on the ropes in the first-half against France in Paris. However, two tries from flanker Martyn Williams, the eventual Six Nations player of the tournament, plus a conversion, three penalties and a dropped goal from outside-half Jones, saw them win an amazing clash 24-18. It was their third victory at Stade de France in four attempts.

A first championship success since 1994 and a first Grand Slam in 27 years was well and truly on. Wales swaggered to a 44-22 triumph over Scotland at Murrayfield, forward Ryan Jones getting them off to a sensational start with a tremendous try. Only Ireland, who could still win the championship and a second successive Triple Crown, stood between Ruddock's men and a famous Grand Slam. Henson put over a dropped goal and a massive penalty either side of a try from Gethin Jenkins. Then a searing break from strike-runner Tom Shanklin put fullback Kevin Morgan over for the deci-

good factor and begin the 2005 Six Nations with a bang.

Wales did; a late and sensational long-range penalty from golden boy Gavin Henson giving them an 11-9 success over England. It was the first time the Red Rose had gone down at the Millennium Stadium. Shane Williams had bagged the Welsh try while Henson

sive try during a 32-20 triumph. It was Ireland's first loss in Cardiff in 22 years. It seemed as if the whole of the country had descended on the Welsh capital as the streets were packed with people celebrating.

Injuries to leading players decimated Wales for the autumn campaign that followed and they weren't a match for New Zealand and South Africa. However, they finished it on a high with their first victory over Australia in 18 years, Shane Williams scoring the vital try during a memorable 24-22 triumph.

But all was not well behind the scenes. There had been claims of discontent – denied publicly by all parties – and unhappiness at the coaching of Ruddock. A 47-13 battering against England at Twickenham didn't help. Neither did the absence of so many of Wales' stars. But they appeared to get the show back on the road with a comfortable 28-18 victory over Scotland at the Millennium Stadium. However, just two days later, Ruddock was on his way amid allegations of player-power.

Australian Scott Johnson, Wales' skills guru, was up-graded to caretaker coach but they failed to win again in the Six Nations, losing to Ireland and

France and becoming the first country to draw at home against Italy.

Llanelli Scarlets coach Gareth Jenkins, the people's choice who had not been deemed good enough two

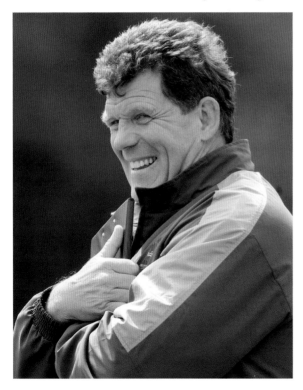

years earlier by the WRU when they parachuted in Ruddock, got the top job, but his experimental team of youngsters went down 2-0 in Argentina.

Things did not improve during the 2007 Six Nations Championship although the cause was hindered initially by injuries. Wales simply did not have the firepower to match Ireland in Cardiff. They were beaten 19-9 and Jenkins promptly decided to rest players against Scotland. It was a mistake as Wales were poor during a 21-9 defeat at Murrayfield. They restored some pride in Paris, out-scoring France 3-2 in tries but going down 32-21 amid a feeling that their opponents were always firmly in control.

Performances were inconsistent, there was a lack of continuity in selection and the nation wasn't much clearer about Wales' tactics under Jenkins when he left than they were at the start of a disappointing 19-month reign.

Worse was to follow as Wales suffered a 23-20 reverse against Italy in Rome, following a 'clock-up'. They were confused over how much time was left and opted to kick a penalty to touch, rather than run it. English referee Chris White controversially blew up for full-time and unhappy Wales had lost again.

There was just one match left to stave off the threat of a Six Nations whitewash and wooden spoon, against neighbours and arch-rivals England at the Millennium Stadium.

With reputations on the line, Wales produced a passionate and determined performance. England were duly dispatched 27-18 with the prodigiously talented Hook going through the scorecard with a try, conversion, four penalties and drop-goal to score 22 of Wales' points.

Wales worked on their fitness before the first of their warm-up matches for the World Cup, against England at Twickenham, but they suffered a record 62-5 humiliation. Jenkins claimed afterwards that England's tactics had surprised Wales and he had fielded a third-choice team. Neither of those assertions found favour with the Welsh public. Jenkins had lost his support base and was never to regain it.

A 27-20 victory over Argentina in Cardiff temporarily lifted the gloom but a comprehensive 34-7 home drubbing against France brought more soul-searching and sent morale plummeting with the World Cup rapidly approach-

DESPAIR, GLORY AND DISBELIEF

RIGHT An ecstatic
Shane Williams after
scoring a try against
France at the 2008 Six
Nations championship

BELOW Training for
the Welsh team with
Warren Gatland

ing. Fans feared the worst as they trailed 17-9 and were on the rack against Canada in their Pool B opener in Nantes. However, 33 points during a devastating 16-minute spell turned the encounter on its head as Wales recovered to win 42-17.

Old foes Australia were next up, in Cardiff, with most regarding it as a group decider. Australia were comfortable 32-20 victors but Wales bounced back from a shoddy start against minnows Japan to win 72-18.

Fiji's victories over Japan and Canada, however, meant their clash with Wales, in Nantes on September 29, was an eliminator for the right to join group winners Australia in the quarter-finals. It was Fiji's World Cup 'final' while Wales seemed to already have one eye on a last eight showdown with eventual champions South Africa.

The clash most expected never materialised with Wales 25-3 down against Fiji after just 25 minutes. Amazingly,

they recovered to lead 29-25 and 34-31, only to throw it away with three minutes left, Fiji prop Graham Dewes condemning them to a 38-34 defeat.

Wales could not complain but the implications were soon apparent with Jenkins being fired by WRU group chief executive Roger Lewis some 15 hours later. It wasn't a surprise because the coach had not capitalised on having a squad of players containing numerous Grand Slam winners. Since Ruddock had departed in February 2006, Wales had won just six out of 23 Tests. It was simply not good enough and drastic action had to be taken.

A new face arrived in the form of Warren Gatland, whose appointment was announced in November 2007 but it was Nigel Davies who temporarily took charge of the side for the 34-12 defeat against a visiting South Africa. Gatland, who had coached numerous club sides and the Irish national team (1998-2001), found himself with the daunting task of trying to boost his players' morale for his first game…the Six Nations opener against England at Twickenham. Trailing 19-6 after an hour thanks to Wilkinson's kicking and a try from Toby Flood, Wales staged an

| THE LITTLE BOOK OF WELSH RUGBY

inspired comeback in the final 20 minutes and tries from Lee Byrne and Mike Phillips helped the visitors record a dramatic 26-19 victory. It was the first time Wales had beaten England on their own patch in 20 years.

Hopes were raised following this result and Gatland's team faced Scotland at the Millennium Stadium a week later in a buoyant mood. Shane Williams grabbed a brace of tries while Hook and Stephen Jones shared the kicking duties in a 30-15 win. Italy were the next visitors and they were summarily dispatched 47-8 with Wales touching down for five tries (two each for Byrne and Shane Williams with Shanklin grabbing his first of the Six Nations campaign). With England beating France in Paris the same day, this left Wales as the only nation who could win the Grand Slam.

Wales' fourth game saw them travel to Ireland to take on the current Triple Crown holders. With the match being played at Croke Park, the home of Gaelic Football, the two sides contested a closely-fought game that saw Wales twice down to 14 men with Phillips and Martyn Williams each spending 10 minutes in the sin-bin. Two O'Gara penalties

against one from Stephen Jones gave the home side a 6-3 lead at half-time but Shane Williams (who had filled in at scrum-half in Phillips' absence) latched onto a pass from Jones in the 51st minute and raced past three Irish players to score the only try of the match. Although Ireland fought back to within a point, a late penalty from substitute Hook

ABOVE Wales players celebrate their Triple Crown victory over Ireland during the Six Nations, March 2008

ensured that it would be the visiting side that emerged triumphant.

Not only did Williams' try help his side claim the Triple Crown courtesy of their 16-12 victory, it also saw him equal Gareth Thomas' record of 40 tries for Wales. It was slight recompense for his countrymen with Wilkinson overtaking Neil Jenkins' record as the all-time leading scorer in the history of international rugby later that day.

So, the scene was set for an emotional weekend in Cardiff on March 15 as Wales welcomed France. The French gave the home side their toughest match of the tournament and the first hour saw the opposing kickers battling it out for supremacy. Hook scored three out of his five penalties while Jean-Baptiste Elissalde registered 100 per cent with his three kicks to leave the match level at 9-9. Then, the mercurial Shane Williams latched onto a mistake by Jauzion, who spilled the ball under pressure from Shanklin. Williams pounced, hacking the ball forward twice before diving on it under the posts to become Wales' greatest try scorer sending the crowd delirious at the prospect of another Grand Slam. Further penalties from Jones and a try from Martyn Williams (after a sensational 80-metre break by Mark Jones) clinched the 29-12 victory and their 10th title.

Shane Williams was named the player of the tournament and his 41st try resulted in his father winning £25,000 from a £50 bet placed almost 10 years previously that his son would one day become the country's leading try scorer.

The euphoria didn't last long, however, as Gatland took his squad to South Africa in June. A dismal showing in the first Test saw the Springboks cruise to a 43-17 victory despite tries from Jamie Roberts and Shane Williams. In the rematch the following week, Wales offered more resistance this time but finished the game still looking for their first victory on South African soil after a 37-21 defeat. Gareth Cooper scored an opportunist try after 20 minutes before Shane Williams scored a wonderful solo effort shortly after the half-hour mark with a dazzling run that saw him weave past five opponents to touchdown in the corner.

While Gatland's first season in charge had seen a turnaround in Wales' fortunes, he had another three years to go on his contract and wanted to build on his initial success. But to do that, he insisted that the Welsh clubs must field more local talent on a regular basis.

"Long-term we have to reduce the amount of foreign players," he explains. "I understand the regional teams wanting to be strong and wanting to compete, but from our point of view we want to compete at international rugby. There are some talented players who we would like to see on the rugby field in regional rugby. Sometimes you have got to go through a little bit of pain with the younger players because you know they are not quite ready. We have tried to support a policy of picking players that are based here and that have stayed here. To continue to do that we have to give those younger players an opportunity."

Welsh rugby fans will be hoping that the regional teams take note of his comments and that further success is just around the corner.

ALSO AVAILABLE

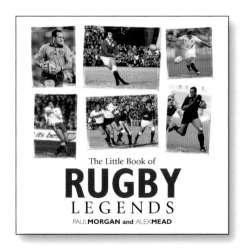

The Little Book of
RUGBY
L E G E N D S
PAUL**MORGAN** and ALEX**MEAD**

Available from all major book shops

The pictures in this book were provided courtesy of the following:

GETTY IMAGES
101 Bayham Street, London NW1 0AG

EMPICS
www.empics.com

RUGBY RELICS
www.rugbyrelics.com

Image Research: Ellie Charleston and Kevin Gardner

Creative Director: Kevin Gardner

Published by Green Umbrella Publishing

Publishers Jules Gammond and Vanessa Gardner

Written by Andy Howell